Simple Puppets You Can Make

Jennifer MacLennan

Sterling Publishing Co., Inc. New York

There are many people who have helped and encouraged me along the way with their support and enthusiasm, as well as with their practical contributions. I owe a debt to them all, but there are some special people who deserve to be named here. My thanks in abundance to Michael Cea, for his help and patience the last time, especially with the Elf, and for his support this time; to Moysha Olshansky, who, though he may not know it, helped to restore my faith in my work; to John Tobias and especially to Dennis Johnson and Larry Nash, for the launch and the encouragement to do it all again; and to a special sister, Juanita MacLennan, whose shared memories inspire me always—here's to the magic attic.

Finally, to Tim Turner, whose support and belief in me have been so unfailingly given, thanks for so many things—especially for teaching me to use the computer! This book is for you.

Jennifer MacLennan is also the author of *Lovable Soft Toys.*

Library of Congress Cataloging-in-Publication Data

MacLennan, Jennifer.
Simple puppets you can make.

Includes index.
1. Puppet making. I. Title.
TT174.7.M23 1988 745.592′24 87-26691
ISBN 0-8069-6816-8

1 3 5 7 9 10 8 6 4 2

Copyright ©1988 by Jennifer MacLennan
Published by Sterling Publishing Co., Inc.
Two Park Avenue, New York, N.Y. 10016
Distributed in Canada by Oak Tree Press Ltd.
% Canadian Manda Group, P.O. Box 920, Station U
Toronto, Ontario, Canada M8Z 5P9
Distributed in the United Kingdom by Blandford Press
Link House, West Street, Poole, Dorset BH15 1LL, England
Distributed in Australia by Capricorn Ltd.
P.O. Box 665, Lane Cove, NSW 2066
Manufactured in the United States of America
All rights reserved

Contents

Introduction

For hundreds of years, people of all ages have been fascinated by puppets. Puppetry is a legitimate and often elaborate theatrical form, but recently puppets have become popular as children's toys. It is with this latter emphasis in mind that this book has been written.

Young children in particular are captivated by puppets; they possess great suspension of disbelief and can accept the actions and words of a puppet as if they were those of a living creature.

The puppets in this book range in complexity from simple finger puppets to increasingly more elaborate hand puppets. Some are traditional three-finger puppets, whereas others are mouth-operated, and still others require the use of five fingers. All are within the skills of the average seamstress, and will provide hours of fun for children whether they manipulate the puppets themselves or watch them being operated by an adult.

· 1 ·
Materials and Techniques

Materials

The puppets in this book are made primarily from fake fur and felt, but some can also be made from alternate fabrics, such as corduroy, velour, or velveteen. In addition to basic fabrics, you'll need:

- cardboard or lightweight flexible plastic for mouth operation;
- good sharp scissors for fabrics, and a separate pair for paper or cardboard;
- sewing machine;
- needles for hand sewing;
- permanent marker;
- good strong glue for attaching features; and
- polyester fibrefill stuffing in small amounts.

Some of the puppets have plastic eyes, purchased from crafts suppliers or notions departments. If plastic eyes are not available in your area or if you would prefer not to use them, you can easily devise some equally effective eyes from felt.

You will notice that some of the puppets are variations on a single design. After making a few of the puppets described in this book, you should be able to use the basic techniques and designs to create your own animals and characters. Don't be afraid to experiment with various fabrics and characteristics.

Techniques

The general directions that follow apply to all of the puppets in this book; you will also find them useful when you are working on your own designs and variations. Read this section very carefully before proceeding with any of the puppets.

PATTERNS: In most cases, full-size patterns are provided for the puppets. These patterns should be traced and mounted on cardboard. This initial step is especially worthwhile if you want to use the patterns more than once, because cardboard patterns are easier to trace around than paper ones. You can use cardboard from a cereal box for this purpose.

LAYOUTS: You will find that the fabric amounts given are usually the minimum amounts for each puppet, and are based on the most economical layouts. No layouts are provided, but it's not difficult to work out your own using the following guidelines. Always cut puppet patterns from a single layer of fabric to avoid distortion. Do not attempt to pin the pattern pieces to the fabric. Instead, trace around them onto the wrong side of the fabric with a marker or dressmaker's pencil. Begin with the larger pieces and then fit the smaller ones in around them. On fur fabric, place each piece so that the nap runs in the direction of the arrows on the pattern pieces. To determine the nap direction, stroke the fabric; if it feels smooth, you are stroking down the nap. Remember to reverse any pieces that are cut in pairs, such as wings and tails. With felt you don't need to worry about grain, so no arrows are provided for felt pieces. Following this method, you should be able to cut according to the most economical layout. Finally, on pieces meant to be cut from ordinary woven fabrics, the arrows should lie along the lengthwise grain as in conventional layouts. (In other words, the arrows should run parallel to the selvages.)

CUTTING OUT: Cut all pieces carefully along traced lines. On fur pieces, avoid cutting through the pile on the front by snipping through the backing only with the point of the scissors.

STITCHING: When stitching puppets, always baste first, and fit the pieces together carefully. This preliminary step is especially important when you are working with fur fabric because it tends to stretch and become distorted during stitching. Carefully fitting the pieces together is the only way to be sure of creating a well-shaped puppet, and it's far better to spend a little extra time at the beginning than to have to rip out the stitching to do it over. Also, it's difficult, if not impossible, to remove faulty stitching from some fur fabrics. Stitch with a fine stitch by machine or hand. *Note:* A ¼-inch seam allowance is provided on all puppets, unless otherwise noted.

TURNING: Clip all corners and trim all curves. Turn the puppet through the opening, being sure to turn small parts such as fingers, noses, snouts, and toes first. You will find a length of dowel or an unsharpened pencil very useful for turning.

STUFFING: Most of the puppets don't require stuffing, and those that do are usually stuffed lightly. You should fill the extremities first, using small pieces of stuffing and pushing them down with a length of dowel or a pencil. When stuffing the heads for three-finger puppets, pack the stuffing firmly but leave some room in the middle to accommodate a finger to manipulate the head.

HAND SEWING: Although most of the sewing is done by machine, at some point you'll need to do some hand sewing—usually to attach some appendage or to close an opening left for stuffing. I use a stitch called a ladder stitch. It's similar to a running stitch, but alternating stitches are made in either side of the fabric (see Illus. 1). When you pull up on the thread, the stitches disappear into the fabric, making the stitching secure and invisible.

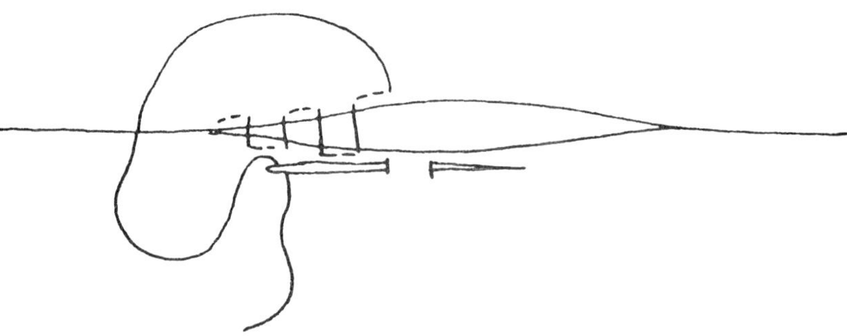

Illus. 1. Ladder stitch

MOUTHS: For mouth-operated puppets, you will need to use a stiff lining of cardboard or lightweight flexible plastic. Cut the piece of cardboard or plastic according to the mouth pattern. Score along the fold line. If you are using cardboard, glue it to a piece of soft interfacing for durability. Spread the inner folded surface of the mouth lining with a generous amount of glue. Then carefully insert the mouth lining into the mouth of the finished puppet, making sure that the glue touches all the surfaces of the mouth and that the lining is in the proper position. This will take some practice, but you will soon become proficient at placing the lining correctly. (For more detailed instructions, turn to page 76.)

CIRCLE TECHNIQUE: In order to make many of the puppets described in this book, you'll need to use the circle technique. This consists of gathering a circle of fabric up into a ball and stuffing it. You can use the ball to form such parts as eyes, noses, and tails. Here's the technique: First, cut out the circle from your fabric. With a double length of thread in a hand needle, run a gathering thread all around the outside edge of the circle. Pull up gently on the thread with the right side of the fabric towards the outside until the circle begins to curl up into a ball. Stuff as you go with plenty of filling, making sure the ball is firm and without ridges. Then pull the thread tight and secure it with a few stitches.

ENLARGING & TRANSFERRING PATTERNS: Patterns for some of the puppets are too large to reproduce in this book. Therefore, they have been reduced by either 25 percent or 50 percent and printed on top of a ¾-inch or ½-inch grid. To enlarge these patterns so that you can use the sizes of the materials given in the directions, buy 1-inch grid paper or make your own. Copy the pattern square by square from the grid in the book onto the large grid paper. After enlarging the pattern this way, cut it out and continue with the instructions.

· 2 ·
Finger Puppets

Finger puppets are the simplest puppets to make, and they can provide children with hours of enjoyment. The finger puppets in this chapter are all variations on a simple shape, designed to fit a single adult finger or two child's fingers. You can easily alter these puppets to create a variety of creatures and animals. Consider the ones presented here as starting points for your own imagination.

Basic Body

All of the finger puppets have the same basic body. To make the body, first cut the body shape from your fabric. Fold about ¼ inch along the bottom straight edge to the wrong side, and hem with a line of machine stitching. Next, fold the body piece in half, with the right sides facing, so that the curved edges meet, and stitch around from the bottom up the center back and around the curved edge. Turn the body right side out and then finish with animal features.

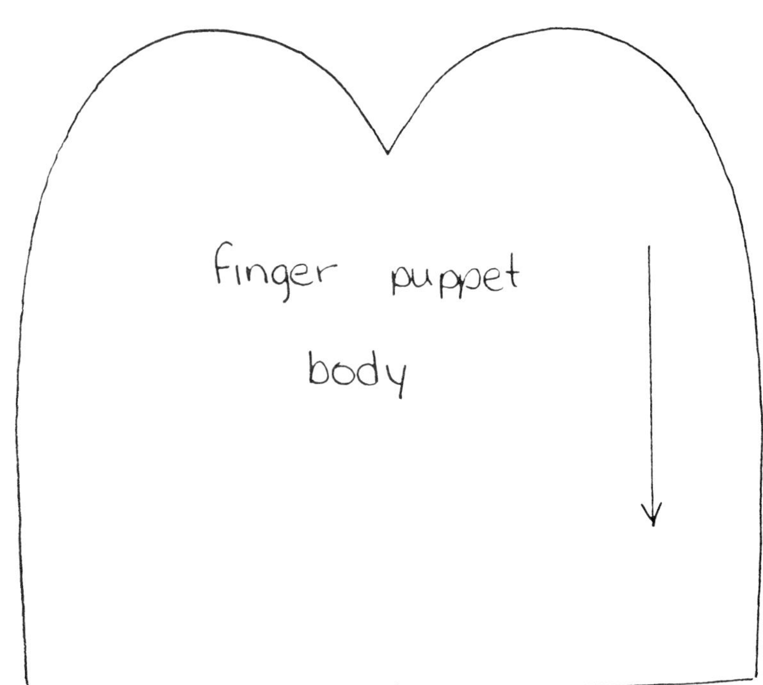

Illus. 2. Basic body pattern for all of the finger puppets

Illus. 3

Bird

Materials: 4″ × 5″ yellow fur fabric
small yellow fluff feather
scraps of orange and black felt

Make the body according to the instructions on page 10, catching the feather in the stitching at the top of the head. Turn. To make the beak, stitch darts in either side and then glue the beak in the middle of the face. Glue the eyes in position above the beak.

Illus. 4

Owl

Materials: 4″ × 5″ grey fur fabric
scraps of red, grey, black, and orange felt

Make the body, following the instructions on page 10. To make the beak, stitch darts in either side and then glue the beak in position in the middle of the face. Glue the eyes in position on the face piece, and glue the face piece to the front of the body above the beak. Stitch darts in the wing pieces; then glue the wing pieces in position on the sides of the body.

Illus. 5

Penguin

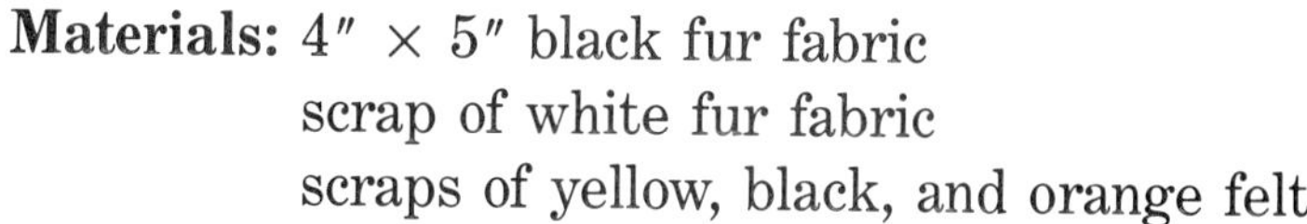

Materials: 4″ × 5″ black fur fabric
scrap of white fur fabric
scraps of yellow, black, and orange felt

Before making the body, glue the breast piece in position and topstitch all around the edge. Now make the body, following the instructions on page 10. Make the beak by stitching darts in either side and then gluing the beak in position in the middle of the face. Glue black pupils to yellow eyes, then the eyes to the face above the beak.

Illus. 6

Monkey

Materials: 4″ × 5″ brown fur fabric
scraps of tan, black, yellow, and white felt

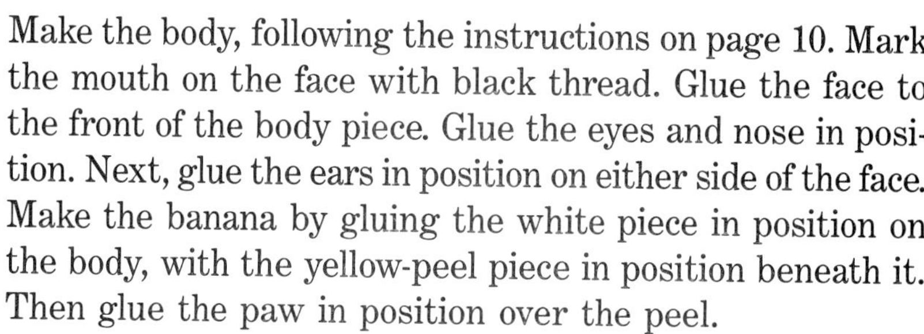

Make the body, following the instructions on page 10. Mark the mouth on the face with black thread. Glue the face to the front of the body piece. Glue the eyes and nose in position. Next, glue the ears in position on either side of the face. Make the banana by gluing the white piece in position on the body, with the yellow-peel piece in position beneath it. Then glue the paw in position over the peel.

Rabbit

Materials: 5″ × 7″ tan fur fabric
scraps of pink, black, white, orange, and green felt

Before making the body, prepare the ears. To make an ear, place two pieces together, with the right sides facing, and stitch all around the curved edges, leaving the straight bottom open; then turn the ear right side out. Now make the body according to the instructions on page 10, leaving the top open. Insert the ears, facing front, into the opening. Flatten out the body so that the middle back seam is in the middle of the body. Stitch across the top of the body, catching the ears in the stitching. Turn. Glue the teeth, nose, and eyes in position on the face. Glue the greens of the carrot in position on the front of the body, and then the carrot on top of the greens.

Illus. 7

Bear

Materials: 5″ × 7″ tan fur fabric
scraps of black, pink, brown, and red felt
tiny amount of polyester fibre stuffing

Make the body, following the instructions on page 10. Make the snout by using the circle technique, described on page 8, using very little stuffing and flattening it out between your fingers. Then stitch the snout in position on the face. Make the ears by gluing the sides together, with the *wrong* sides facing. Glue the ears in position on the sides of the head. Glue the nose and tongue to the snout, and the bow tie beneath it. Glue black pupils to brown eyes, and then the eyes to the face.

Illus. 8

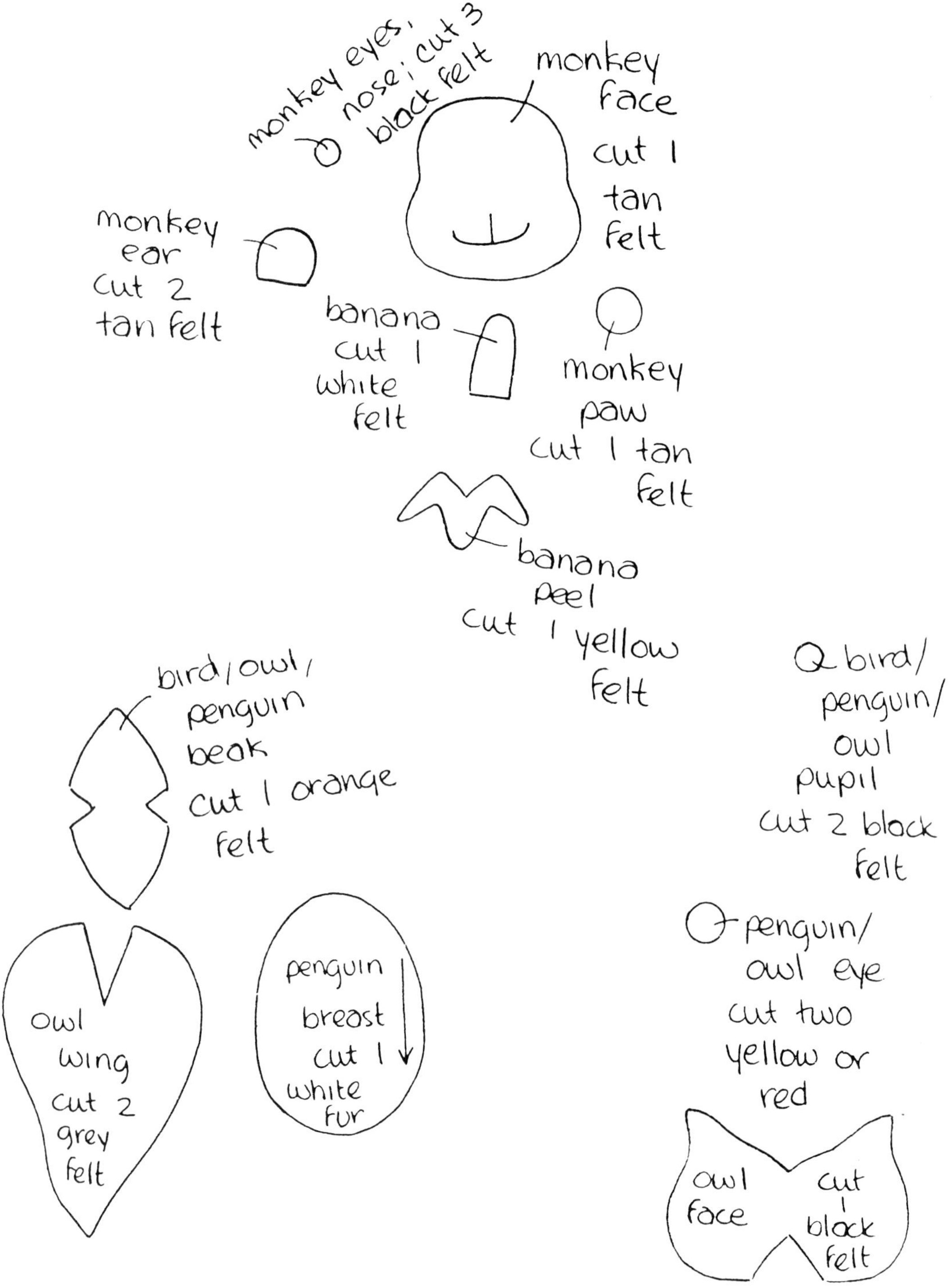

Illus. 9. Additional patterns for the Monkey, Bird, Owl, and Penguin

Illus. 10. Additional patterns for the Rabbit and Bear

· 3 ·
Five-Finger Puppets

The three five-finger puppets presented in this chapter are somewhat unusual in their operation, and require some practice to be manipulated effectively, but they are fascinating in the lifelike quality of their movements and their realistic posture. All three are based on the same fundamental shape, which you can alter to make other creatures.

Muriel Mouse

Illus. 11

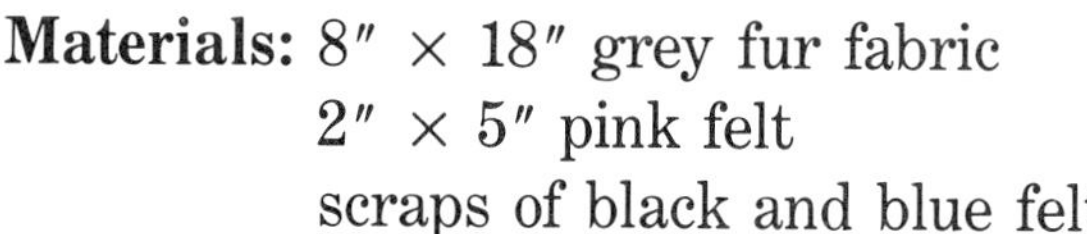

Materials: 8″ × 18″ grey fur fabric
2″ × 5″ pink felt
scraps of black and blue felt

EARS: Prepare the ears by stitching the ear and ear lining pieces together in pairs, with the right sides facing, leaving the straight edge open. Then turn the ears right side out and set them aside.

TAIL: Fold the tail in half lengthwise, with the right sides facing, and stitch, leaving one short end open. Turn right side out. Beginning from the closed end, stitch down the length of the tail with a ladder stitch (see page 8), alternating the stitches in either side of the tail. Pull up on the thread so that the tail will curl up. Fasten off at the open end and then set the tail aside.

BODY: Place the ears (with their right sides facing the right side of the body) in position, facing forward, in the darts on the sides of the head. Stitch the darts, catching the ears in the stitching. Baste the tail in position on one side of the lower back of the body. Stitch the body, with the right sides facing and matching all edges, from the nose (point A) to the base (point B), catching the tail in the stitching. Flatten the body out. Now, stitch the underbody to the body, with their right sides facing, and matching all edges and points A, leaving the bottom open between the notches. Turn the mouse right side out. Then make a narrow hem on the bottom of the body.

FACE: Glue the black nose in position. Glue the pupils to the eyes, and then the eyes in position on the face.

Rupert Rabbit

Materials: 8″ × 18″ white fur
scraps of pink and black felt
small amount of polyester fibre stuffing

EARS: Make the ears by stitching them together in pairs, with their right sides facing, leaving the straight bottom edge open. Turn. Glue the ear linings in position on the ears; then topstitch all around the edge through all the thicknesses.

Illus. 12

BODY: Make the body according to the directions for the mouse's body in the preceding project, but omit the tail. Before attaching the underbody, baste the teeth in position on the underbody piece at point A. Then catch the teeth in the stitching when you attach the underbody to the body.

TAIL: Make the tail by using the circle technique, explained on page 8. Then attach it to the lower back of the rabbit's body.

FACE: Finish according to the face instructions for the mouse.

Illus. 13

Benjamin Beaver

Materials: 8″ × 16″ brown fur fabric
4″ × 5″ brown felt
scraps of black, tan, or orange felt

EARS: Follow the instructions for the rabbit's ears in the preceding project, but omit the linings.

CLAWS & FEET: To make a claw, place two claw pieces together, with the wrong sides facing, and topstitch along the lines indicated on the pattern. Slash between the "fingers." Fold the feet along the indicated fold lines, and topstitch near the folded edge to form the webbing.

BODY: Baste the claws and teeth in the indicated positions on the underbody. To make the body, follow the instructions for the mouse's body on page 17, but omit the tail and leave an opening between D and E. Fold the legs so that the center seams meet, and insert the feet, facing up, into the opening. Then stitch across the opening, catching the feet in the stitching. Do not hem yet.

TAIL: Topstitch a crisscross pattern on one tail piece with gold, tan, or orange thread. Stitch both tail pieces together, with the right sides facing, leaving it open along the straight edge. Turn and press flat. Attach the tail to the bottom back of the body; then hem around the edge of the body's opening.

FACE: Finish according to the face instructions for the mouse.

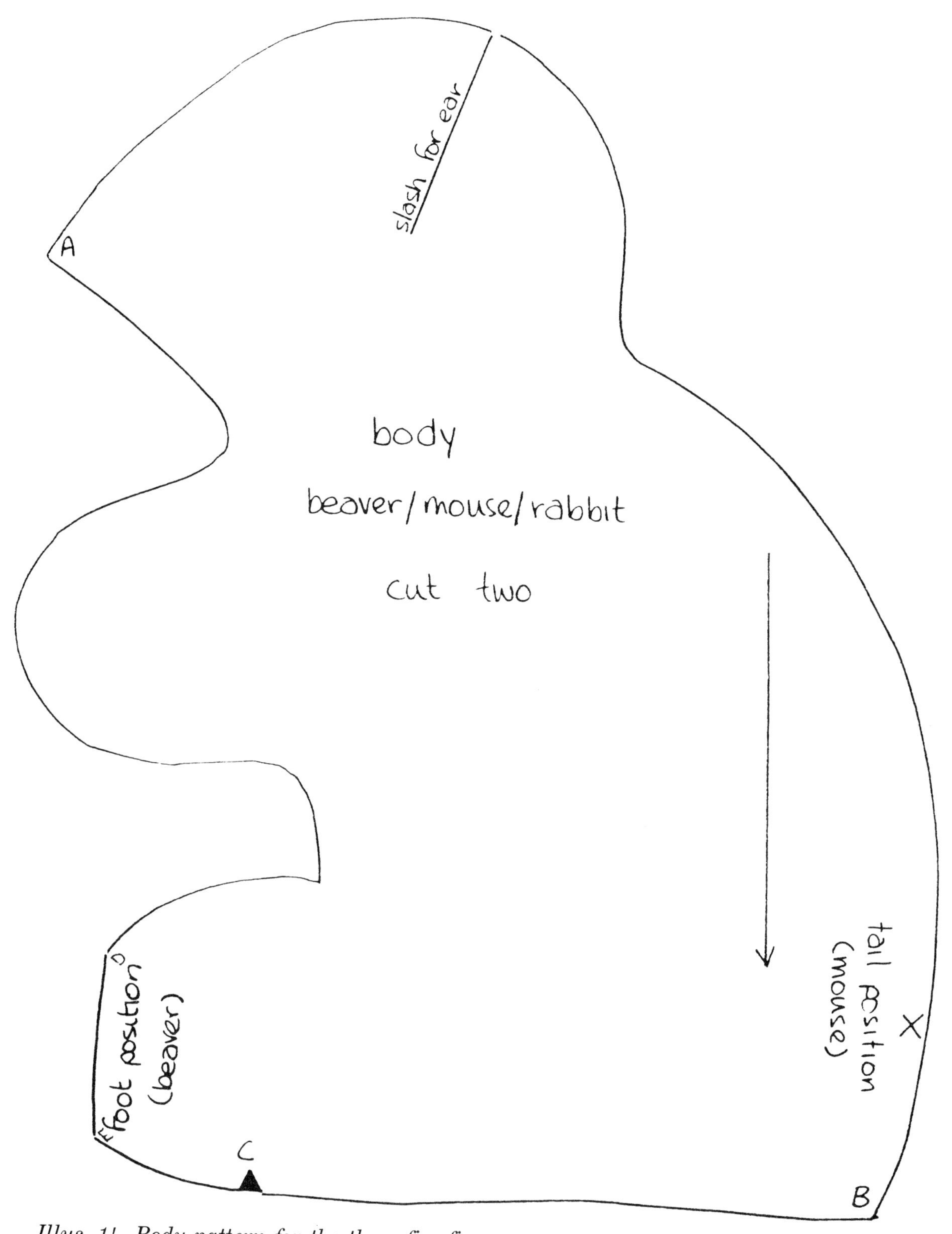

Illus. 14. Body pattern for the three five-finger puppets

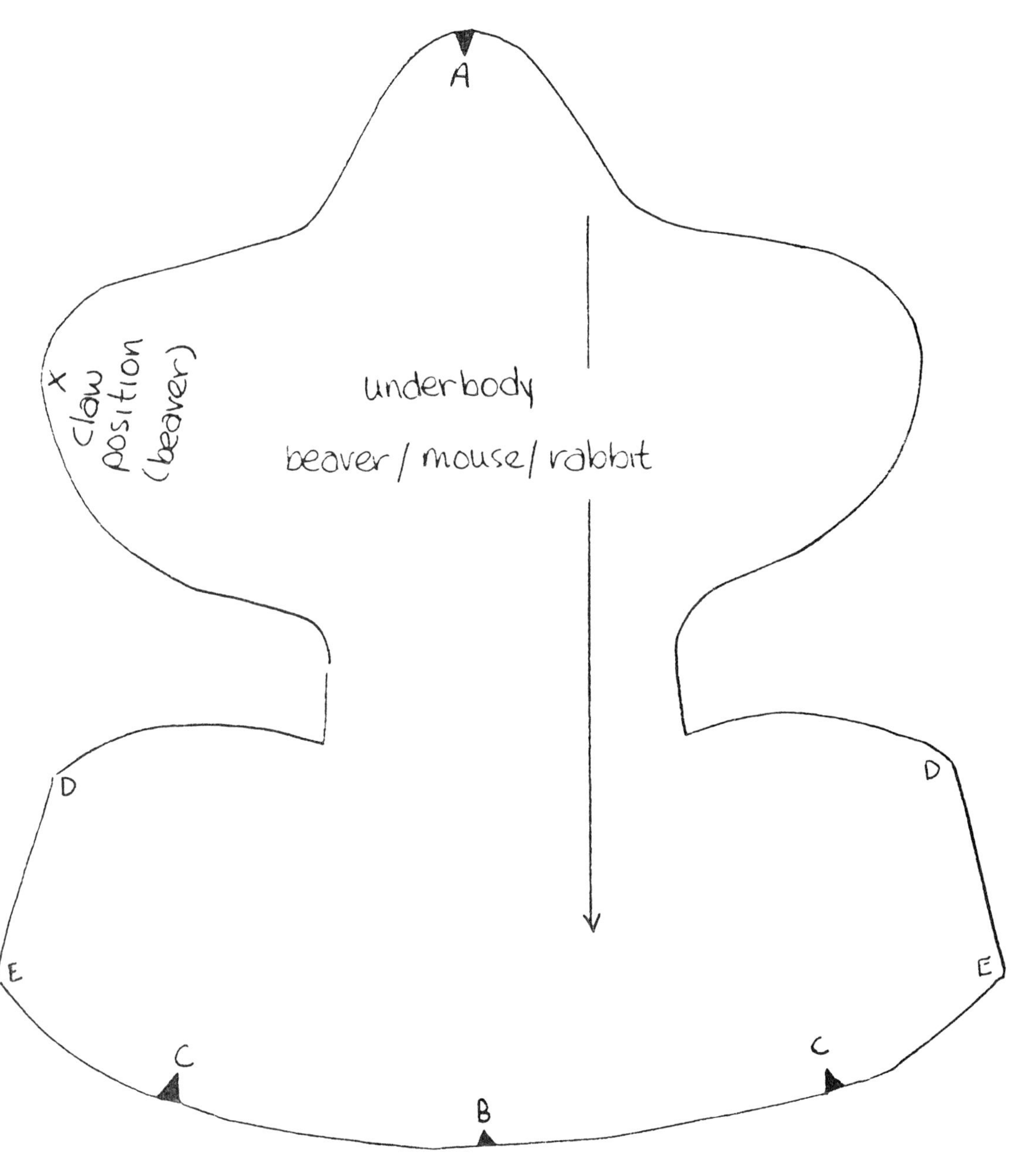

Illus. 15. Underbody pattern for the three five-finger puppets

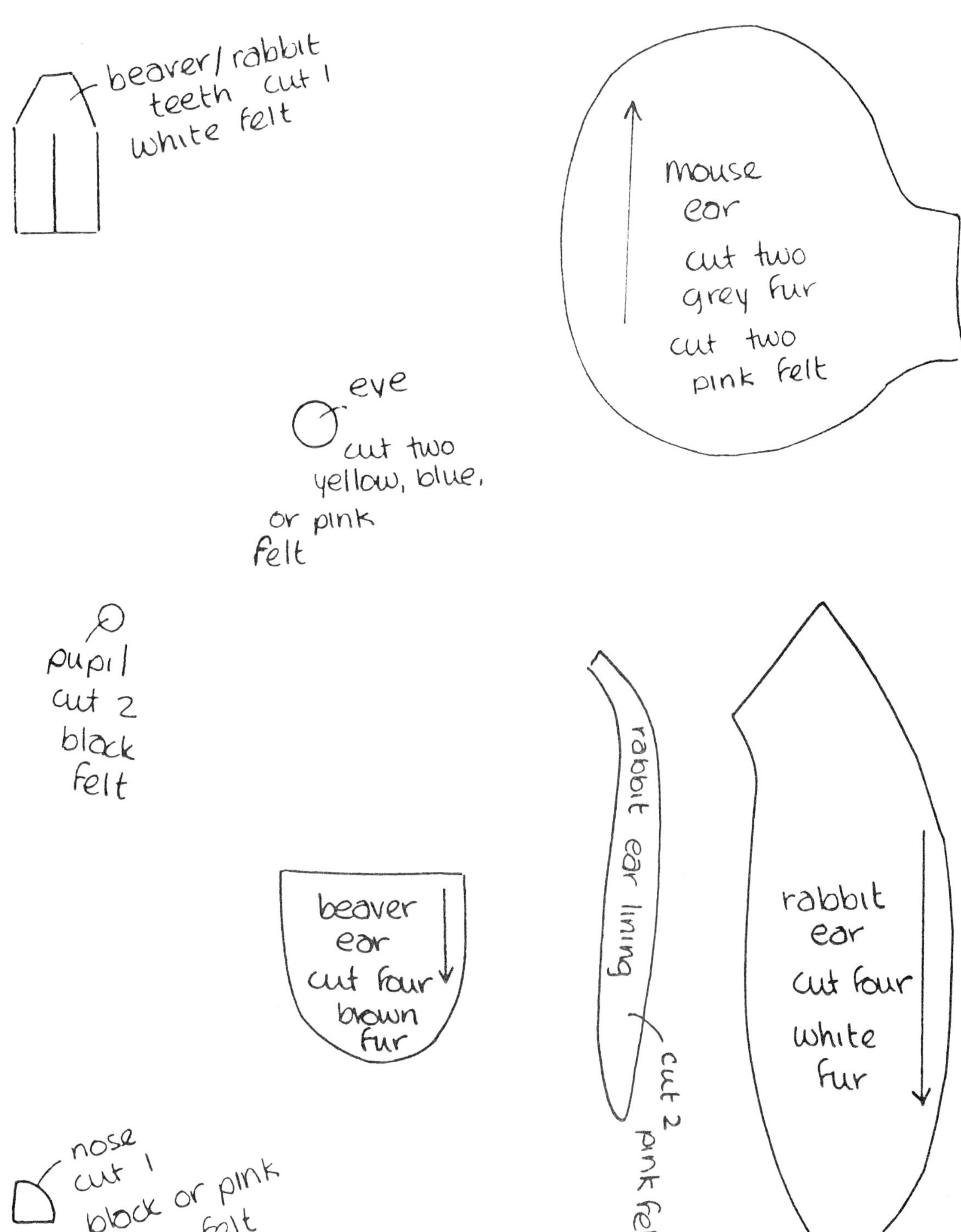

Illus. 16. Ear, nose, eye, and teeth patterns

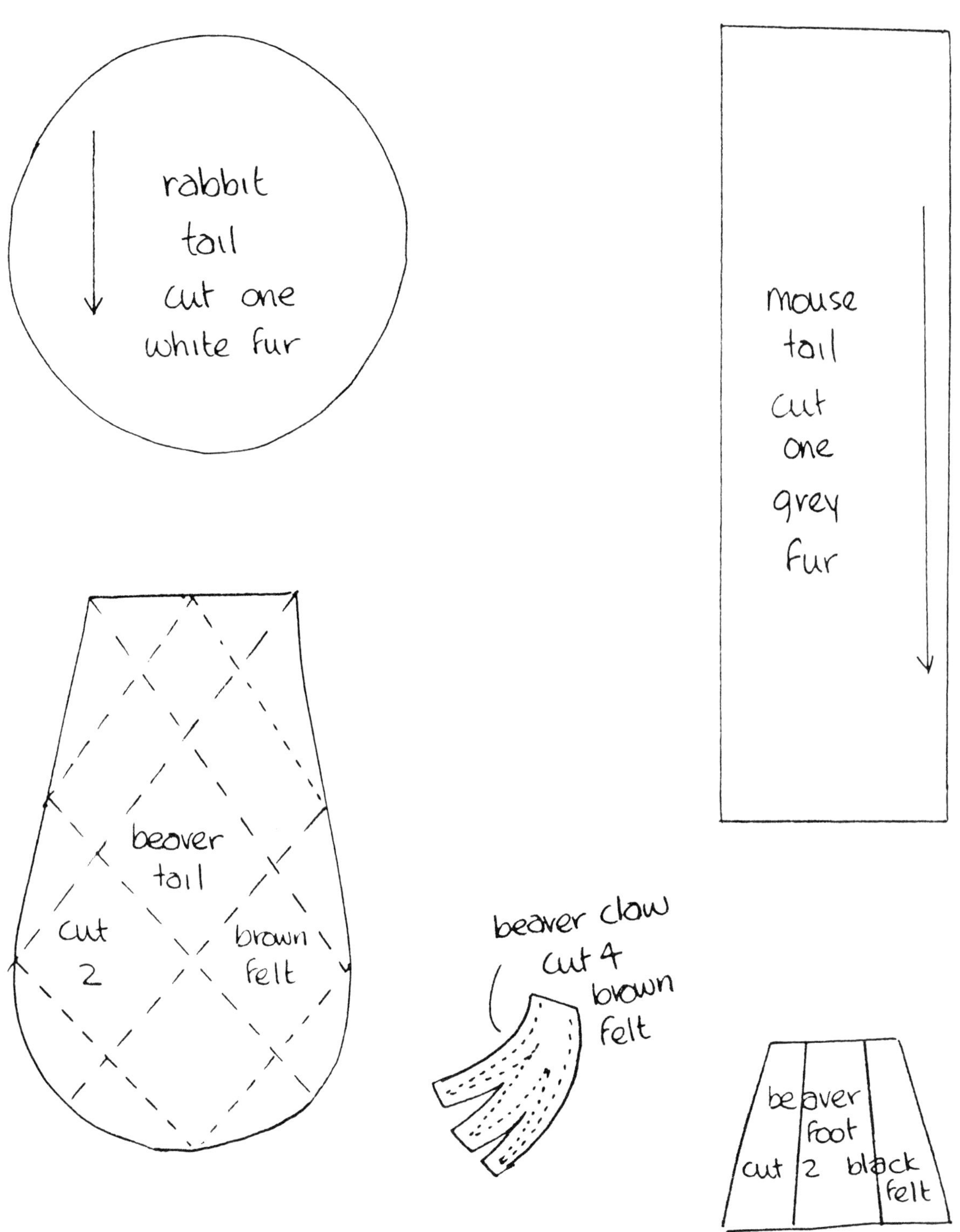

Illus. 17. Tail, claw, and foot patterns

· 4 ·
Three-Finger Puppets

The three-finger puppet is the most common type of puppet, and one of the easiest for children to manipulate. The fascination we have in these puppets lies in their ability to interact with their environment; for example, they can pick things up and touch each other. The three-finger puppets in this chapter will fit the average adult hand, but can also be successfully operated by children. You can alter the basic design to produce a number of different characters and creatures; those presented here are only a few of the possibilities. Read the following instructions and the general directions in Chapter 1 before proceeding.

Basic Instructions

BODY: Baste the two body pieces together, with the right sides facing. Machine-stitch around the outer edge, leaving it open at the bottom. Clip the curves. Turn the body right side out and then set it aside.

HEAD: Stitch the dart at the top and bottom of each head piece. If the puppet has ears, baste them in place on the head front, as indicated on the pattern, matching all raw edges. Stitch around the outer edges of the head pieces, with the right sides facing, leaving it open at the neck and catching the ears in the stitching line. Then turn right side out. The heads on these puppets are fully stuffed and attached to a neck piece that extends into the middle of the head. Stuff the head firmly, leaving a space up the middle that is large enough to accommodate one adult finger.

To attach the head to the neck, first place the body on your hand. With one finger extended into the neck, push the neck of the body into the space made in the stuffing of the head. Tuck the raw edges of the head under and then hand-stitch the head securely to the neck, keeping your finger inside the neck to avoid stitching it closed. If you find it difficult to sew the head to the neck while keeping one hand inside the body, insert a narrow broom handle or similarly shaped object into the neck to keep the stitching from catching the neck closed.

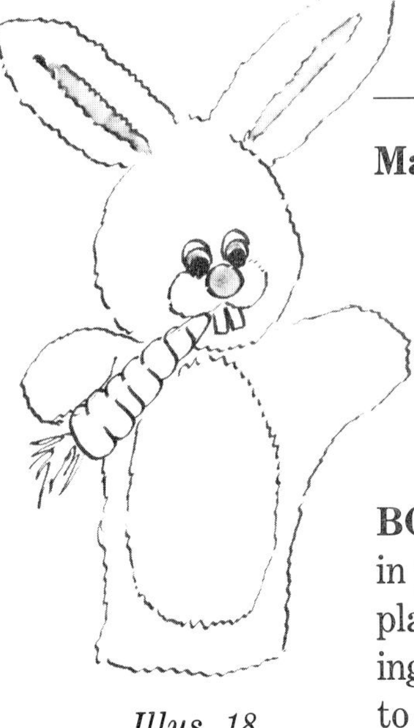

Illus. 18

Herbert Hoppmann Rabbit

Materials: 22″ × 14″ brown fur fabric
2″ × 5″ pink felt
6″ × 6″ white fur fabric
3″ × 3″ green felt
5″ × 5″ orange felt
scraps of white and black felt
polyester fibre stuffing

BODY: First, place the wrong side of the stomach piece in position on the right side of one body piece and baste in place. Next, appliqué it to the body piece by machine-stitching all around the outer edge. Then finish the body according to the basic instructions on page 23.

EARS: Sew the ear pieces together in pairs, with the right sides facing, leaving it open at the bottom. Turn them right side out, but do not stuff them. Glue the ear linings in position on the ears, as indicated on the pattern. Topstitch around the edge of the ear linings, stitching through all thicknesses. Then set the ears aside.

TEETH & SNOUT: Glue two teeth pieces together, with the *wrong* sides facing. Topstitch, following the dotted lines on the pattern. Slash between the teeth. Then place the teeth and snout in position on the right side of one head piece. Glue the snout in place and then topstitch around the edge, catching the teeth in the stitching line.

HEAD: Prepare the head as indicated in the basic instructions on page 23.

FACE: Make the nose by using the circle technique (refer to page 8); then glue or stitch it to the front of the face at the top of the snout piece. Glue or appliqué black pupils to pink irises, and then the pink irises to the whites of the eyes. Now glue or appliqué the eyes in position on the face.

TAIL: Make the tail according to the circle technique on page 8. Then apply it to the body back the way you applied the nose to the face, positioning it approximately 1 inch from the bottom.

CARROT: Fold the carrot in half lengthwise. Stitch down the side to the point, leaving the curved top open. Turn the carrot right side out. Stuff. Slash strips about 3 inches deep into the green square, creating a fringe. Roll the uncut bottom edge up and secure it. Run a gathering thread around the top of the carrot. Pull up and insert the rolled edge of the fringe into the end of the carrot so that the fringe hangs down. Then fasten securely.

Celia Chicken

Materials: 22″ × 14″ white fur fabric
5″ × 2″ orange felt
10″ × 4″ red felt
scrap of black felt
polyester fibre stuffing

Illus. 19

BODY: Make the body according to the basic instructions on page 23.

HEAD: Make the head according to the basic instructions on page 23, but ignore the directions regarding ears.

FACE: Glue the two top and two bottom beak pieces together, with the wrong sides facing; then topstitch along the outer edges. Stitch the beak pieces in place on the head front, starting with the bottom beak. Topstitch around the edge of the wattle piece and then stitch in position below the beak. Make the comb by gluing two comb pieces together, with the wrong sides facing, and then topstitch all around top edge. Stitch the comb in position on top of the head. Glue the eye dots in position on the face.

Illus. 20

Beatrice Bluebird

Materials: 22″ × 14″ blue fur fabric
5″ × 2″ orange felt
scrap of black felt
polyester fibre stuffing
small blue feather fluff

Make the bird according to the instructions for the chicken in the preceding project, but ignore the instructions for the wattles and comb. Instead, insert a small feather fluff in the middle of the head before stitching the head pieces together, catching the fluff in the seam line of the head.

Timothy the Honey Bear

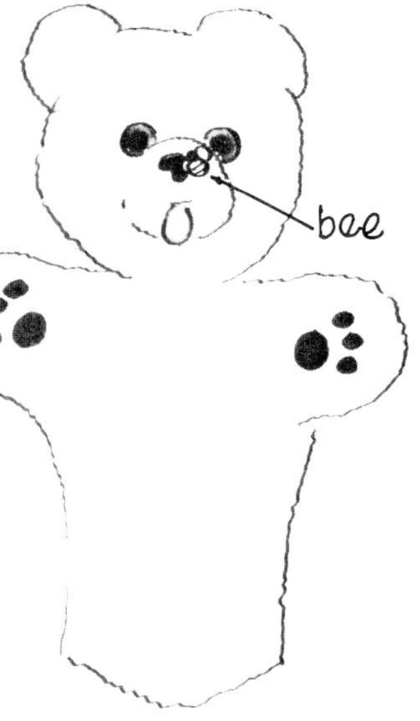

Illus. 21

Materials: 22″ × 16″ light-brown fur fabric
scraps of brown, red, yellow, white, and black felt
1 pair of brown plastic lock-in eyes, 15mm
polyester fibre stuffing
small piece of black Velcro fastening tape

BODY: Make the body, following the basic instructions on page 23. Then glue the paw pads in the positions indicated on the body pattern.

EARS: Stitch the ear pieces together in pairs, with the right sides facing, leaving the bottom edge open. Then turn the ears right side out and set them aside.

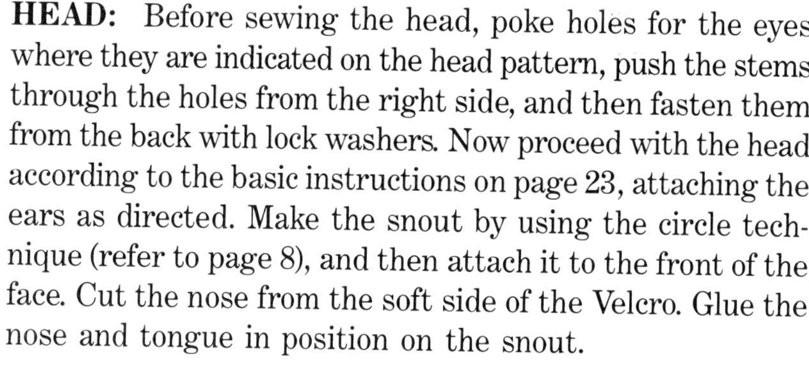

HEAD: Before sewing the head, poke holes for the eyes where they are indicated on the head pattern, push the stems through the holes from the right side, and then fasten them from the back with lock washers. Now proceed with the head according to the basic instructions on page 23, attaching the ears as directed. Make the snout by using the circle technique (refer to page 8), and then attach it to the front of the face. Cut the nose from the soft side of the Velcro. Glue the nose and tongue in position on the snout.

BEE: Make the bee's body of yellow felt, using the circle technique. Make the stripes on the body with black thread, wound tightly two or three times around the body. Glue the wings in position on the bottom of the body and the head in position on the front of the body. Cut the base from the "hook" side of the Velcro and then glue it securely to the bottom of the bee.

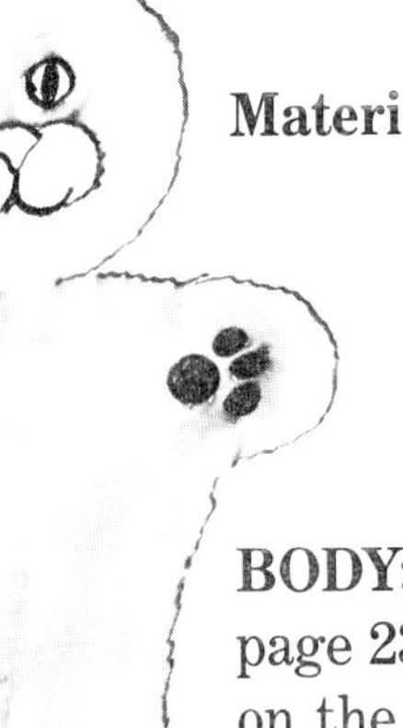

Illus. 22

Purdey the Cat

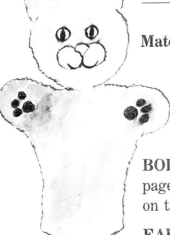

Materials: 22″ × 14″ grey fur fabric
scraps of pink and black felt
scrap of white fur fabric
1 pair of plastic cat eyes, 15mm
polyester fibre stuffing

BODY: Make the body, following the basic instructions on page 23. Then glue the paw pads in the positions indicated on the body pattern.

EARS: Stitch two ear pieces together in pairs, leaving it open at the bottom. Turn the ears right side out and then set them aside.

HEAD: Glue the snout piece in position on the face and then topstitch around the edge. After poking holes for the eyes where indicated on the head pattern, insert the eyes, pushing the stems through from the front and securing them in the back with lock washers. Finish the head according to the basic instructions on page 23.

FACE: Glue the mouth piece to the snout where indicated. Then glue the pink nose piece in position at the top of the snout, covering the mouth.

Illus. 23

Lovable Leopold Lion

Materials: 22″ × 13″ bright-gold fur fabric
6″ × 6″ white fur fabric
6″ × 11″ medium-pile brown fur
scraps of orange, brown, green, and black felt
polyester fibre stuffing

TAIL: Stitch the tail tip to the tail, with the right sides facing, along A-B. Fold the tail in half lengthwise, with the right sides facing, and stitch from the curved end along the long edge, leaving an opening at the end. Now turn the tail right side out.

BODY: Apply the stomach piece the way it's applied for the rabbit on page 24. Then make the body following the basic instructions on page 23. Make a small slit where it's indicated on the back of the body, and then poke the raw end of the tail through from the right side. Stitch the slit closed, catching the tail in the stitching.

EARS: Make the ears the same way they are made for the bear on page 27.

FACE & HEAD: Glue the snout in position on the face piece, and then topstitch all around the snout near the edge. Glue the face in position on the head front; then topstitch around the edges. Make the head according to the basic instructions on page 23, attaching the ears as directed.

EYES & NOSE: Glue the orange nose piece in position on the face front. Glue the brown nose tip over the end of the nose. Glue black pupils to green eyes, and then glue the eyes to the face. For greater security, you can hand-stitch all the features in position.

Santa Claus

Materials: 25″ × 13″ red fur fabric
6″ × 11″ medium-pile white fur fabric
small amounts of black, green, pink, hot-pink, and yellow felt
6″ × 10″ off-white or beige fur fabric
1 pair of plastic moving eyes, 12mm
1 gold jingle bell for hat
polyester fibre stuffing

Illus. 24

BODY: Before making the body, stitch the hands, with the right sides facing, to the ends of the arms along A-B. On the front of the body, glue the fur strip in position vertically; then glue the belt across the body at the bottom of the fur trim, and the buckle in place on top of the belt. You can also stitch these pieces in position, if you wish. Now proceed with the body according to the basic instructions on page 23.

HEAD: Glue the face in position on the head front and secure it by topstitching all around it, near the edge. Finish the head following the basic instructions on page 23.

HAT: Bind the lower curved edge of the hat with short fur by folding the fur in half lengthwise, with the wrong sides together, over the curved edge of the hat. Stitch along the edge of the folded piece, catching the curved edge of the hat in the stitching, so that the fur forms a trim for the hat. Fold the hat into a cone shape, with the right sides facing, and then stitch the back seam from the wide end to the point. Turn the hat right side out and then stitch a jingle bell onto the tip. Glue and stitch the hat in position on the head; then fold the hat over and secure it with small stitches.

FACE: Make the nose using the circle technique on page 8. Glue and stitch the nose to Santa's face, just above the beard. Then glue the eyes in position to either side of and slightly above the nose.

Illus. 25

Mischievous Michael C. Elf

Materials: 25″ × 13″ green fur fabric
6″ × 11″ white medium-pile fur fabric
6″ × 12″ pink felt
5″ × 5″ green felt
scraps of yellow, black, and hot-pink felt
1 long green fluff feather
1 pair of plastic moving eyes, 12mm
red thread
polyester fibre stuffing

BODY: Before making the body, stitch the pink hands, with the right sides facing, to the ends of the arms along A-B of the body piece. On the front of the body, glue the black felt strip for the belt across the middle. Then glue the buckle in position. Now make the body according to the basic instructions on page 23.

EARS: Stitch the ears together in pairs, with the right sides facing, leaving the straight edge open. Turn the ears right side out and press them flat with your fingers. Then set them aside.

HEAD: Place the face in position on the head front. Secure the face by topstitching all around it, near the edge. Matching raw edges, baste the ears in position on the sides of the head. Proceed with the head, as described in the basic instructions on page 23, and then secure it to the body.

FACE: Make the mouth by embroidering it in position with red thread. Make the nose using the circle technique on page 8. Glue and stitch the nose in position in the middle of the face. Then glue the eyes in place to either side of and slightly above the nose.

HAT: With the right sides facing, fold the hat so that the back seam edges meet. Stitch from C to D. Refold the hat so that the back seam is in the middle, and stitch dart E-F. Turn the hat right side out and then fold the flaps up along the fold line indicated on the pattern. Glue the plume under one flap and then secure the flaps in place with a dab of glue. Now glue or stitch the hat in position on the head.

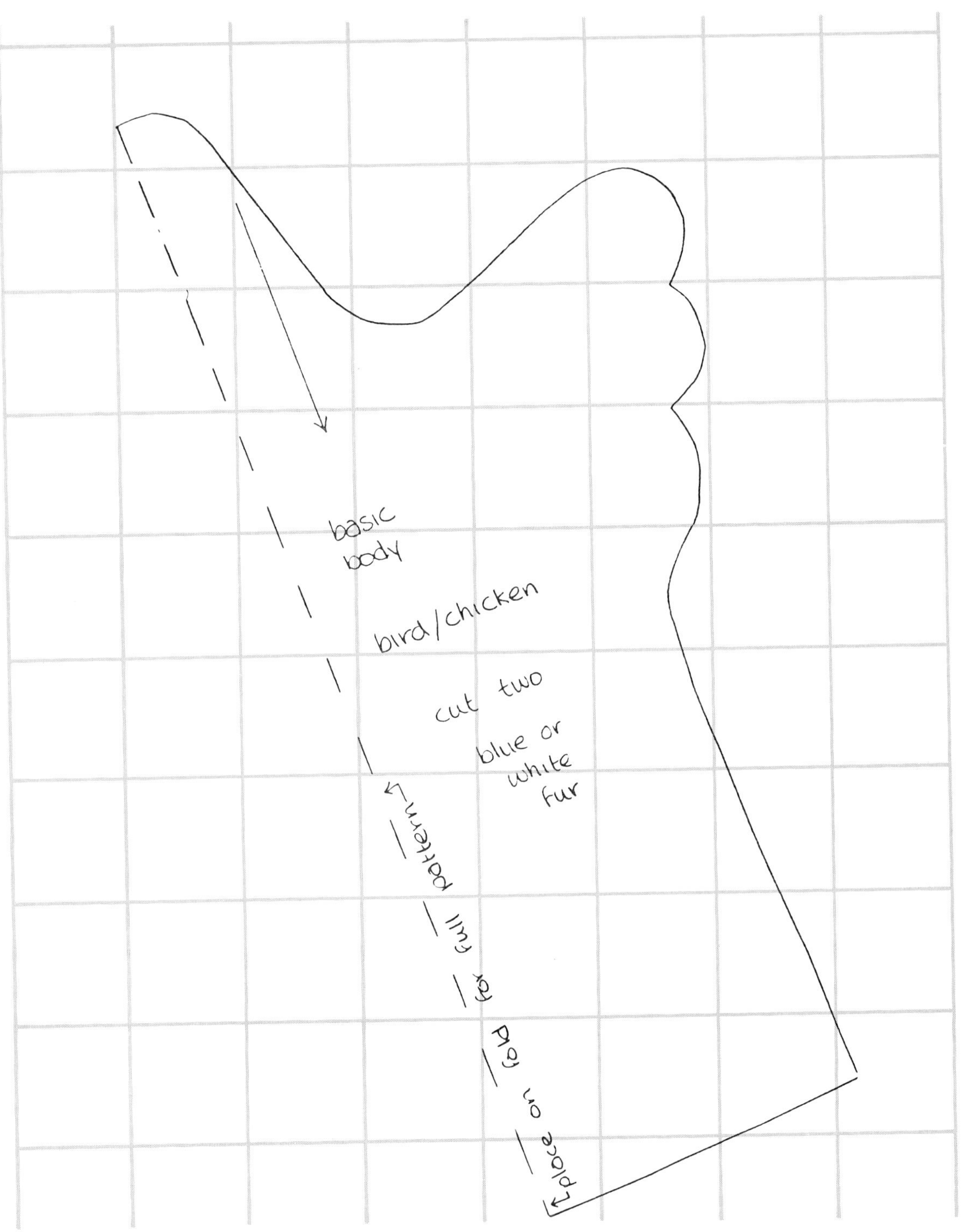

Illus. 26. Basic body pattern for Beatrice Bluebird and Celia Chicken (75 percent of its original size)

This is Mischievous Michael C. Elf with his plastic moving eyes (*see page 30)*, cuddly Uriel Unicorn (*page 49*), and hairy Harry Monster (*page 94*). Both the elf and the unicorn are three-finger puppets; the monster, as you might guess, is a mouth puppet.

A

Little white Rupert Rabbit (*page 17*) is a five-finger puppet; Herbert Hoppmann Rabbit (*page 24*) is a three-finger puppet; and Muriel Mouse (*page 16*), holding Herbert's carrot, is a five-finger puppet. Three-finger puppets are noted for their ability to interact with their environment. What makes five-finger puppets special is their lifelike posture and movements.

Beatrice Bluebird (*page 26*), Dangerous Dan (*page 45*), and Celia Chicken (*page 25*) are three-finger puppets. As with all the puppets in this book, you can alter the basic design according to your own imagination.

Here's Purdey the Cat (*page 28*), Loretta Bird (*page 83*), Timothy the Honey Bear (*page 27*), and the Monkey (*page 12*). Both the cat and the bear are three-finger puppets, the bird is a mouth puppet, and the little monkey is a finger puppet. Simple to make, finger puppets are designed to fit one adult finger or two child's fingers. Mouth puppets are especially fun to use since they can "talk."

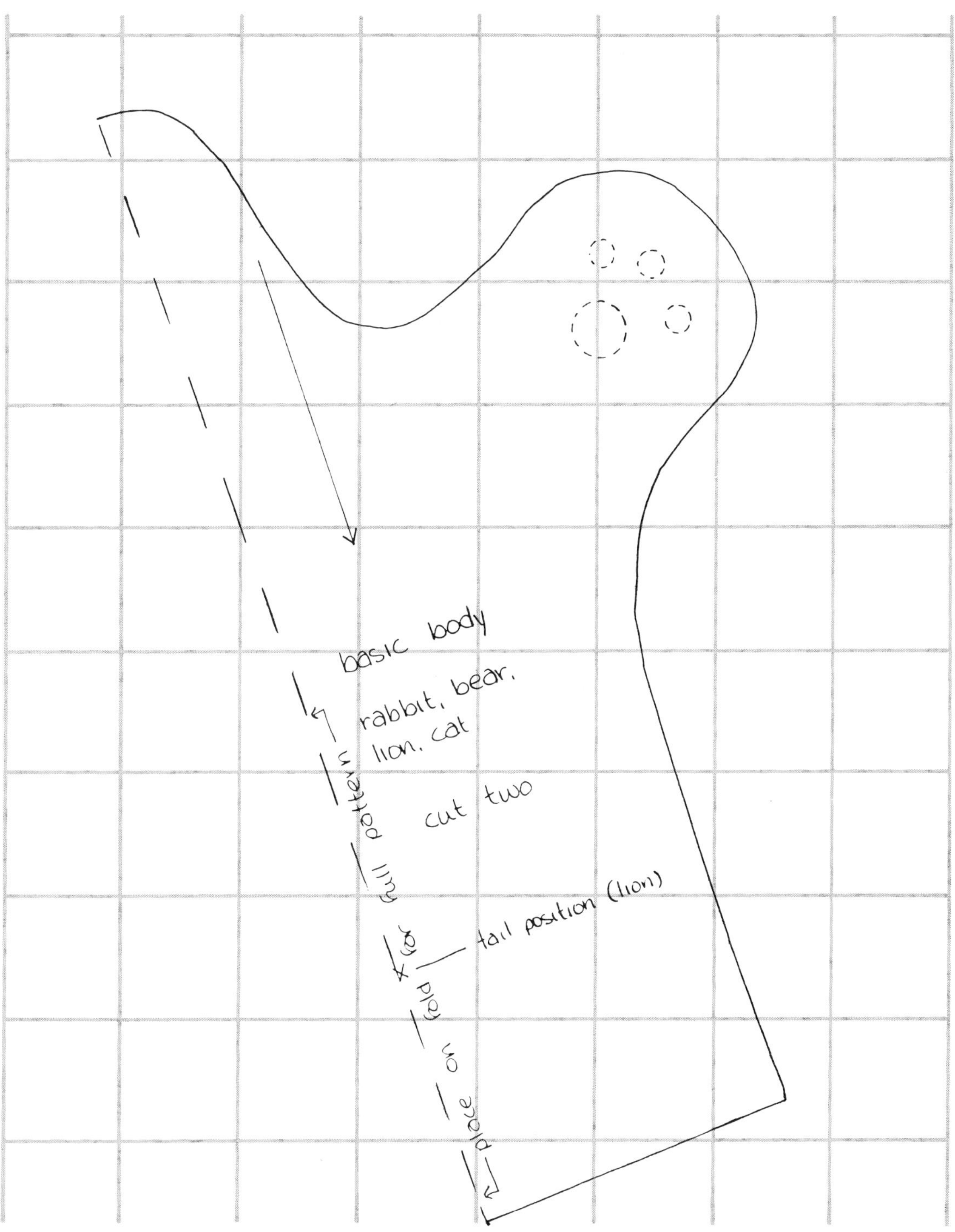

Illus. 27. Basic body pattern for Herbert Hoppmann Rabbit, Timothy the Honey Bear, Lovable Leopold Lion, and Purdey the Cat (75 percent of its original size)

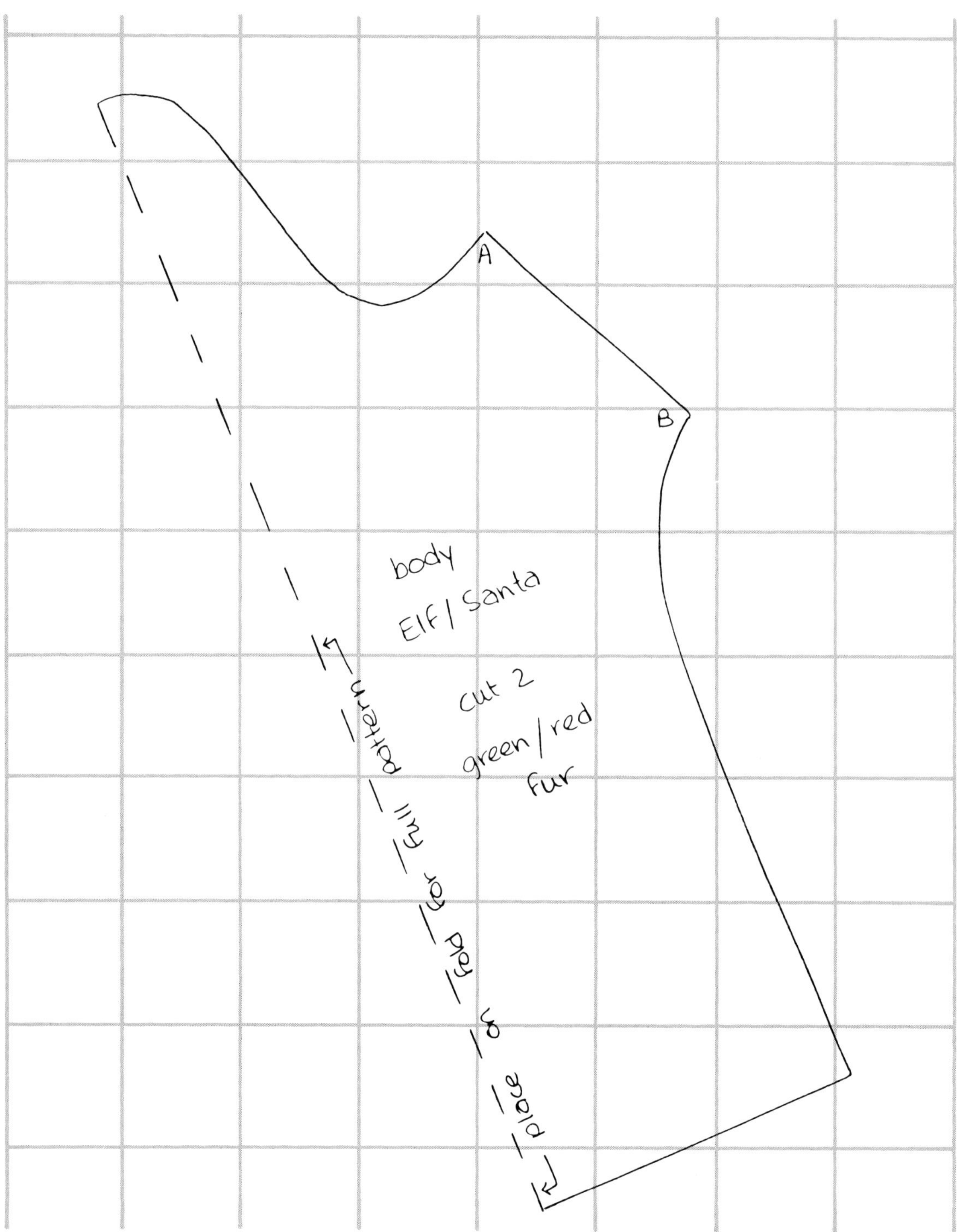

Illus. 28. Body pattern for Mischievous Michael C. Elf and Santa Claus (75 percent of its original size)

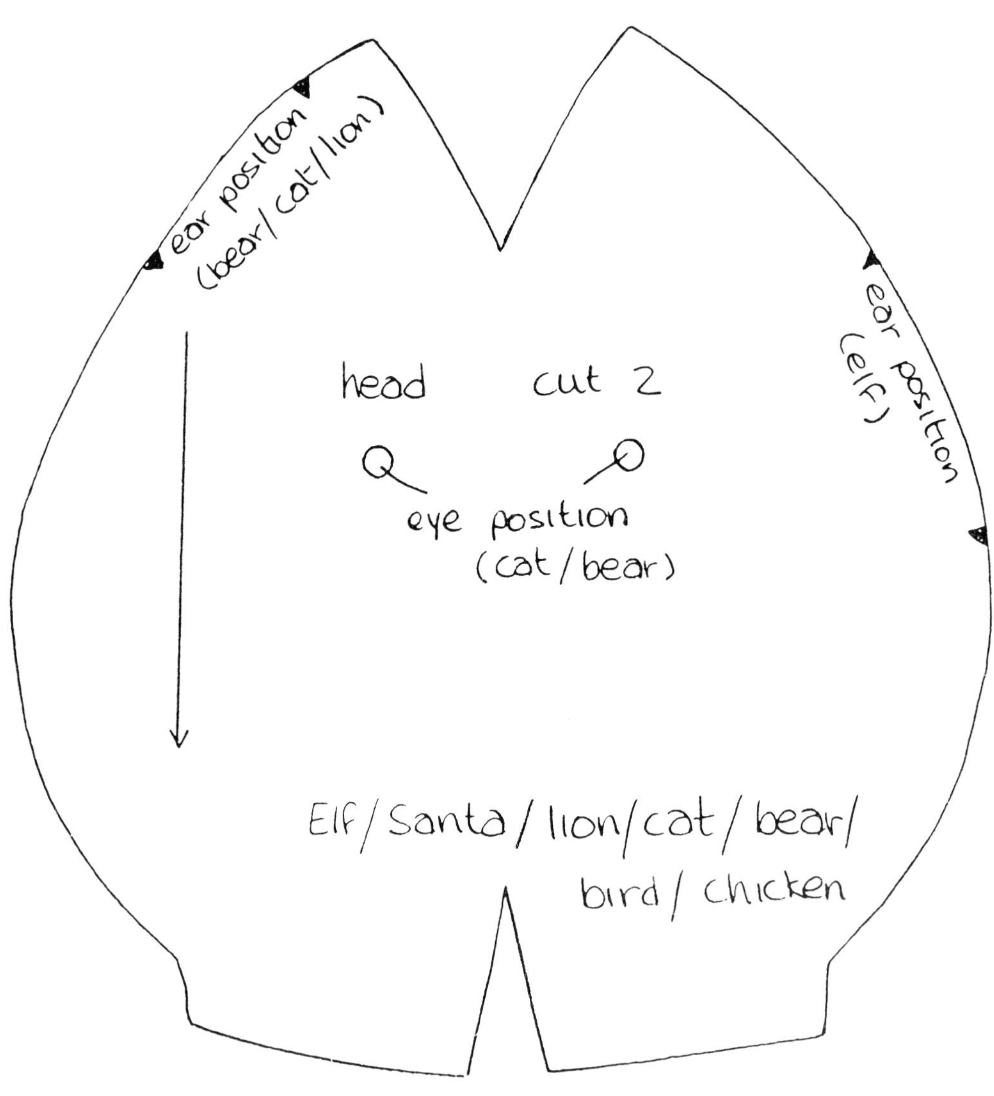

Illus. 29. Head pattern for Mischievous Michael C. Elf, Santa Claus, Lovable Leopold Lion, Purdey the Cat, Timothy the Honey Bear, Beatrice Bluebird, and Celia Chicken

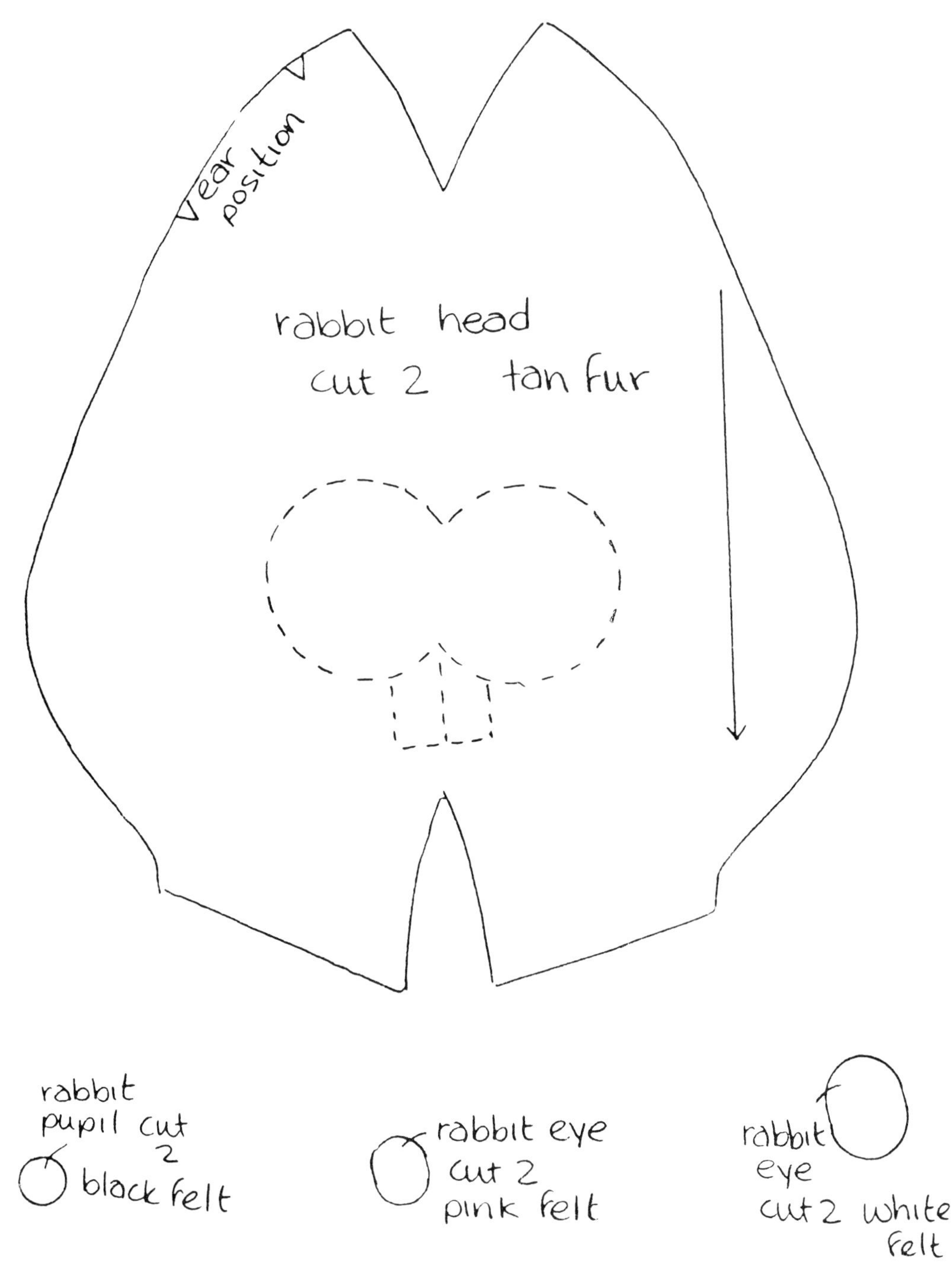

Illus. 30. Head and eyes patterns for Herbert Hoppman Rabbit

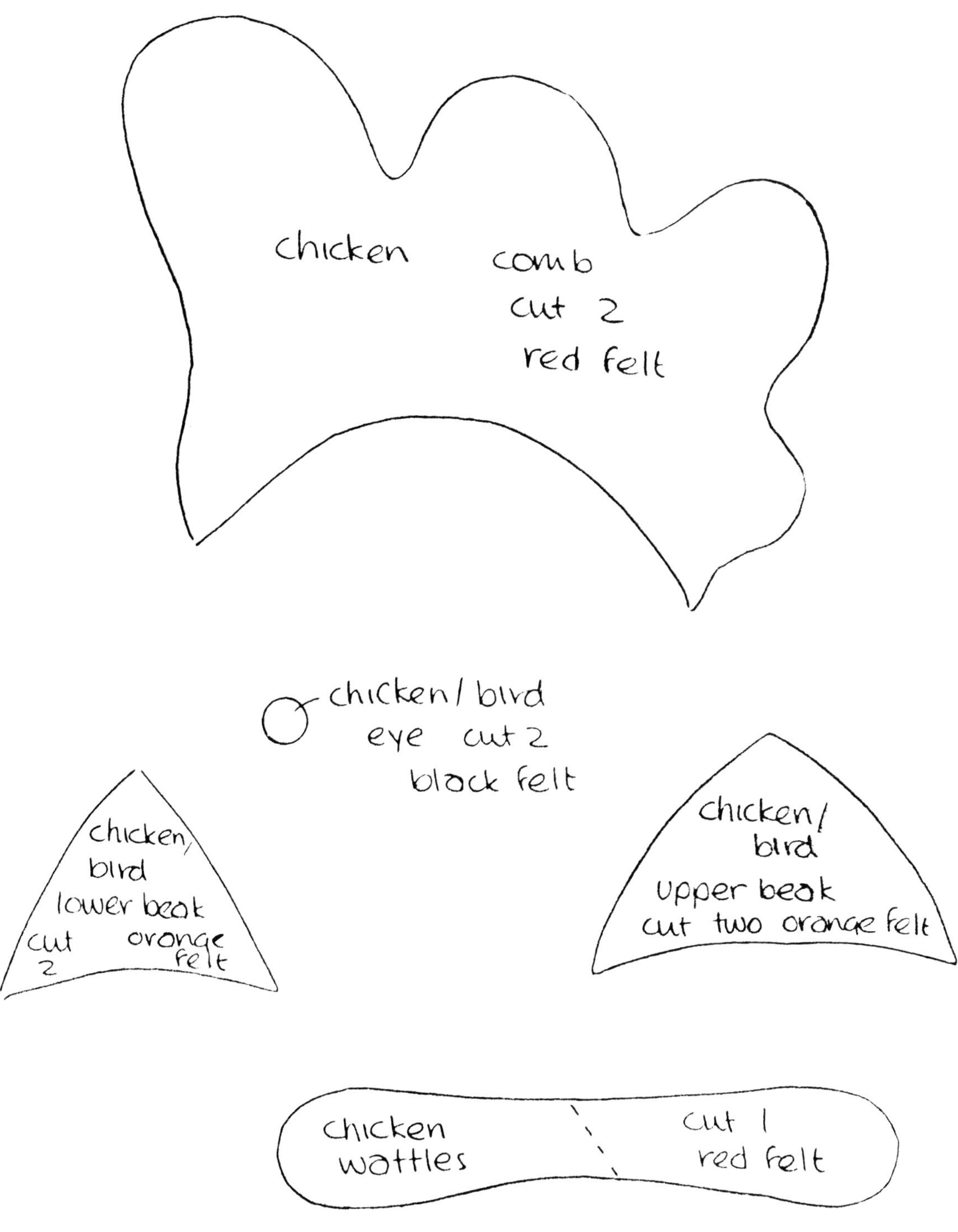

Illus. 31. Additional patterns for the Chicken and Bluebird

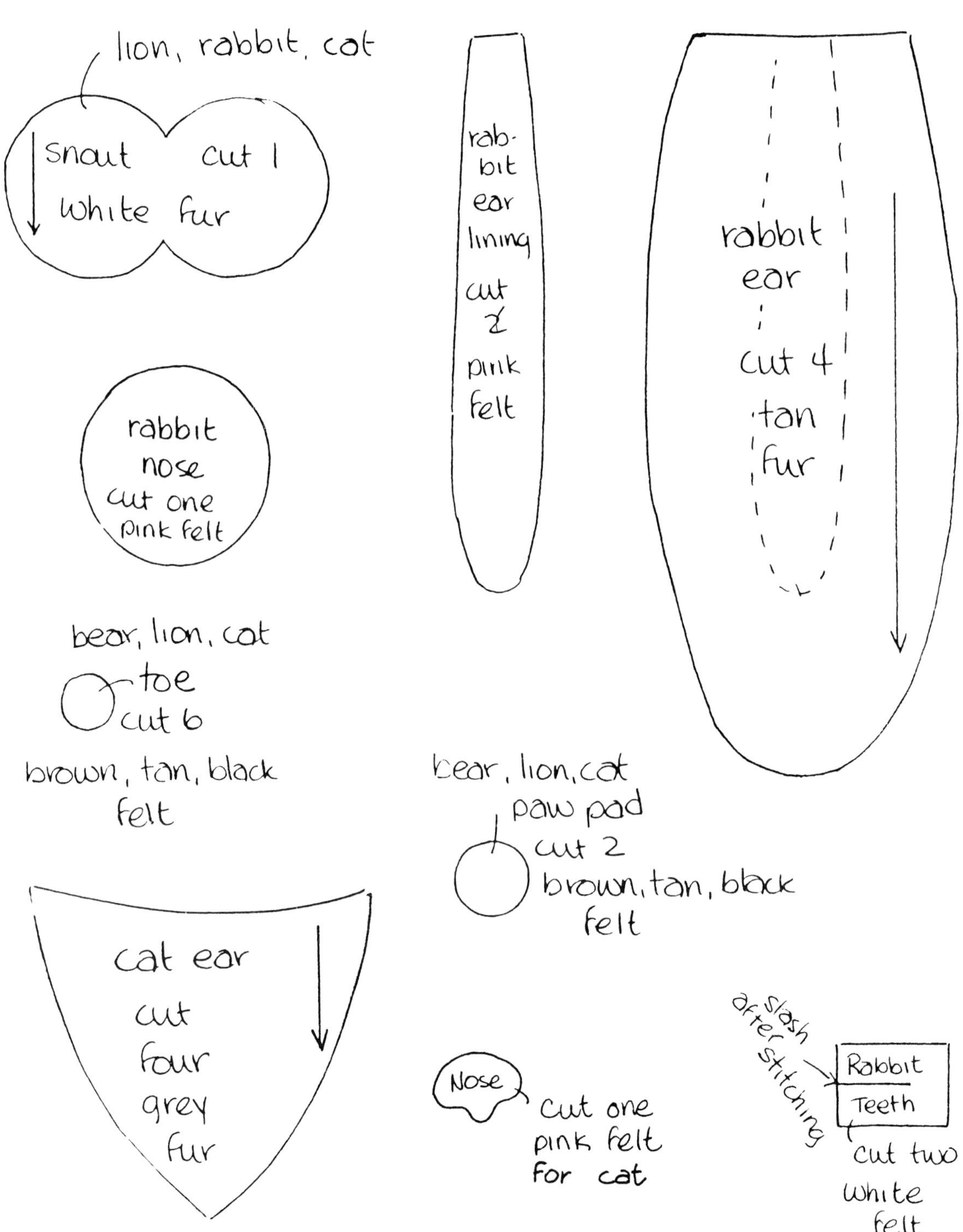

Illus. 32. Additional patterns for the Bear, Lion, Cat, and Rabbit

Illus. 33. More patterns for the Bear, and patterns for the Bee on his nose

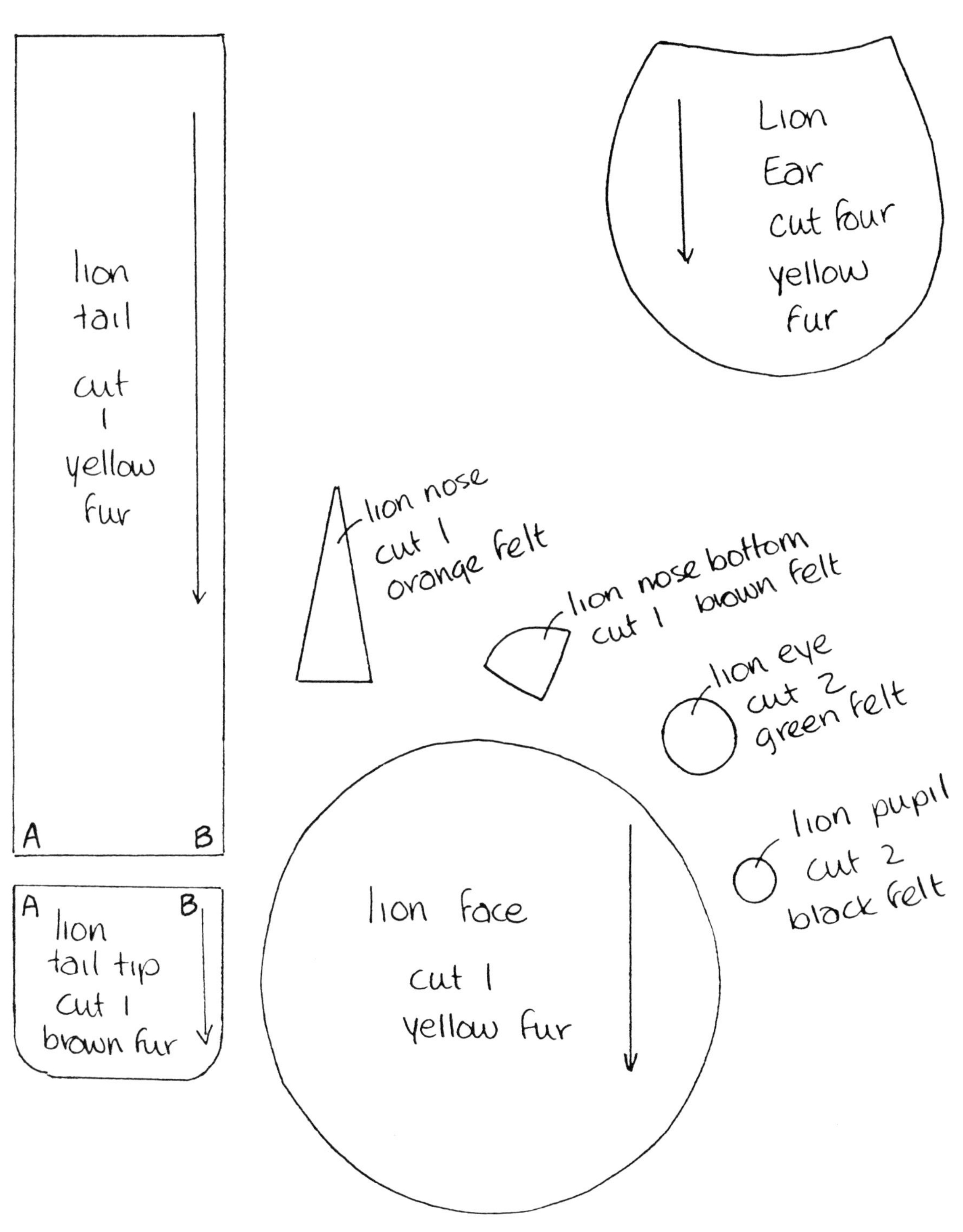

Illus. 34. More patterns for the Lion

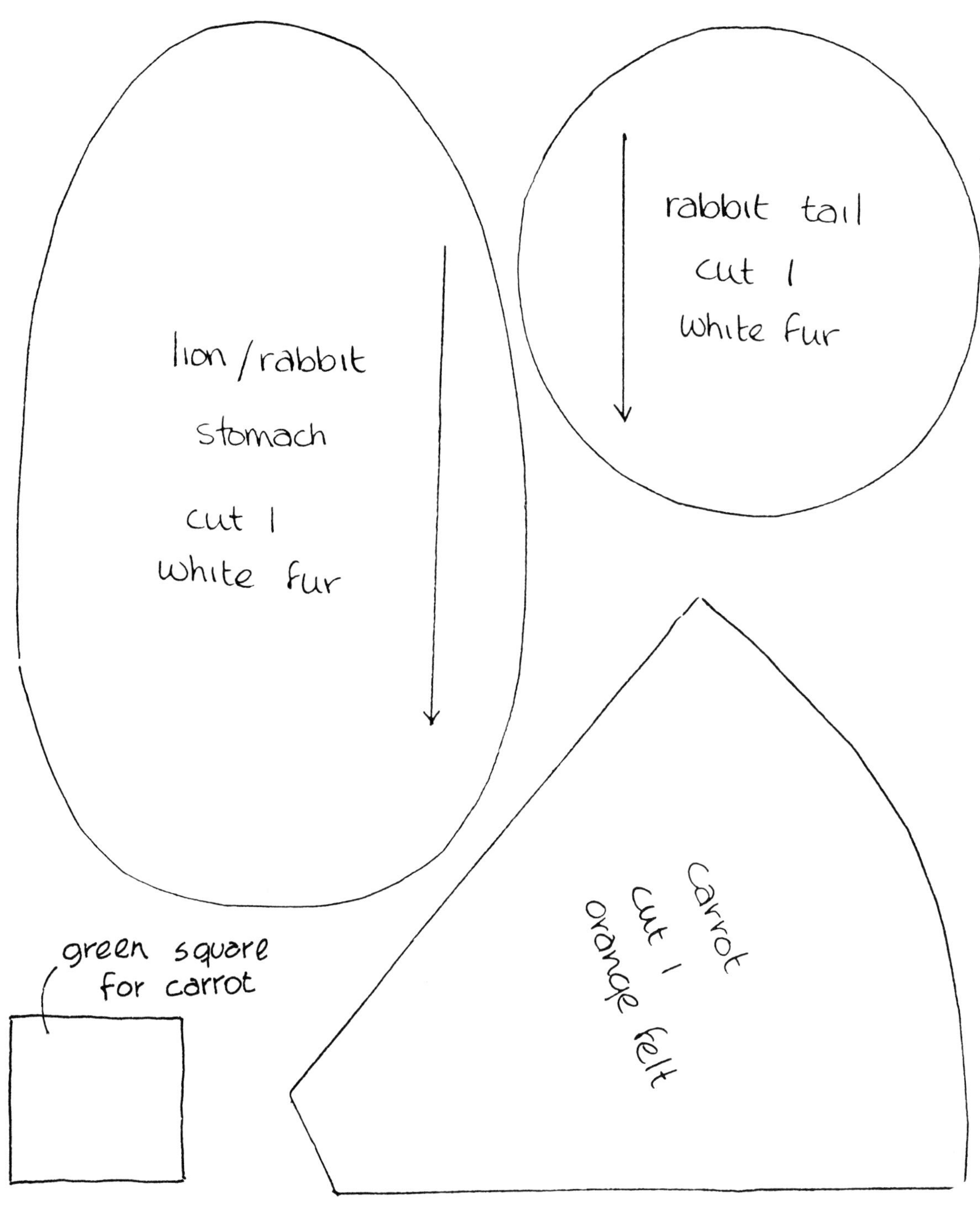

Illus. 35. More patterns for the Lion and Rabbit

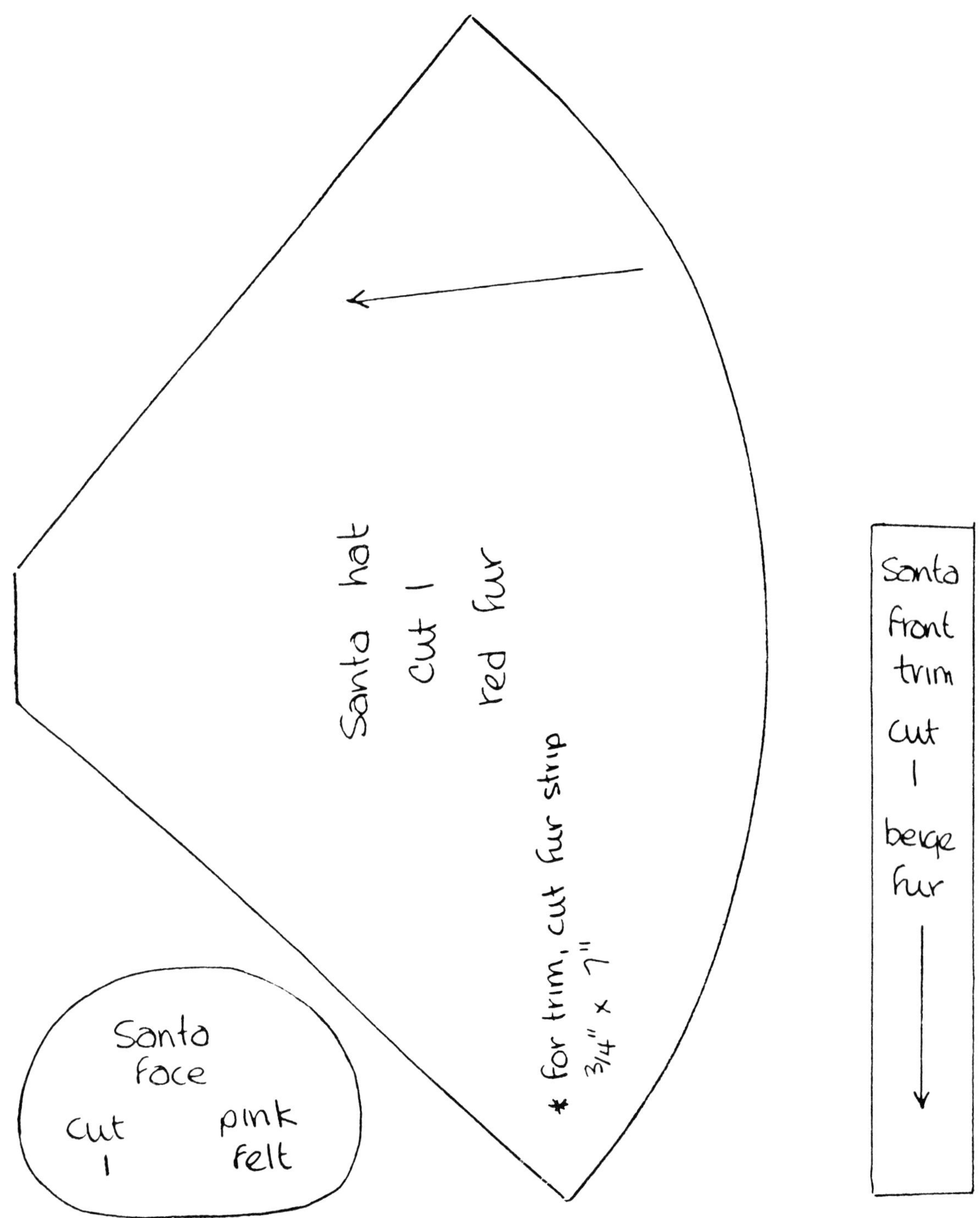

Illus. 36. Patterns for Santa's face, hat, and front trim

Illus. 37. More patterns for Santa and the Elf

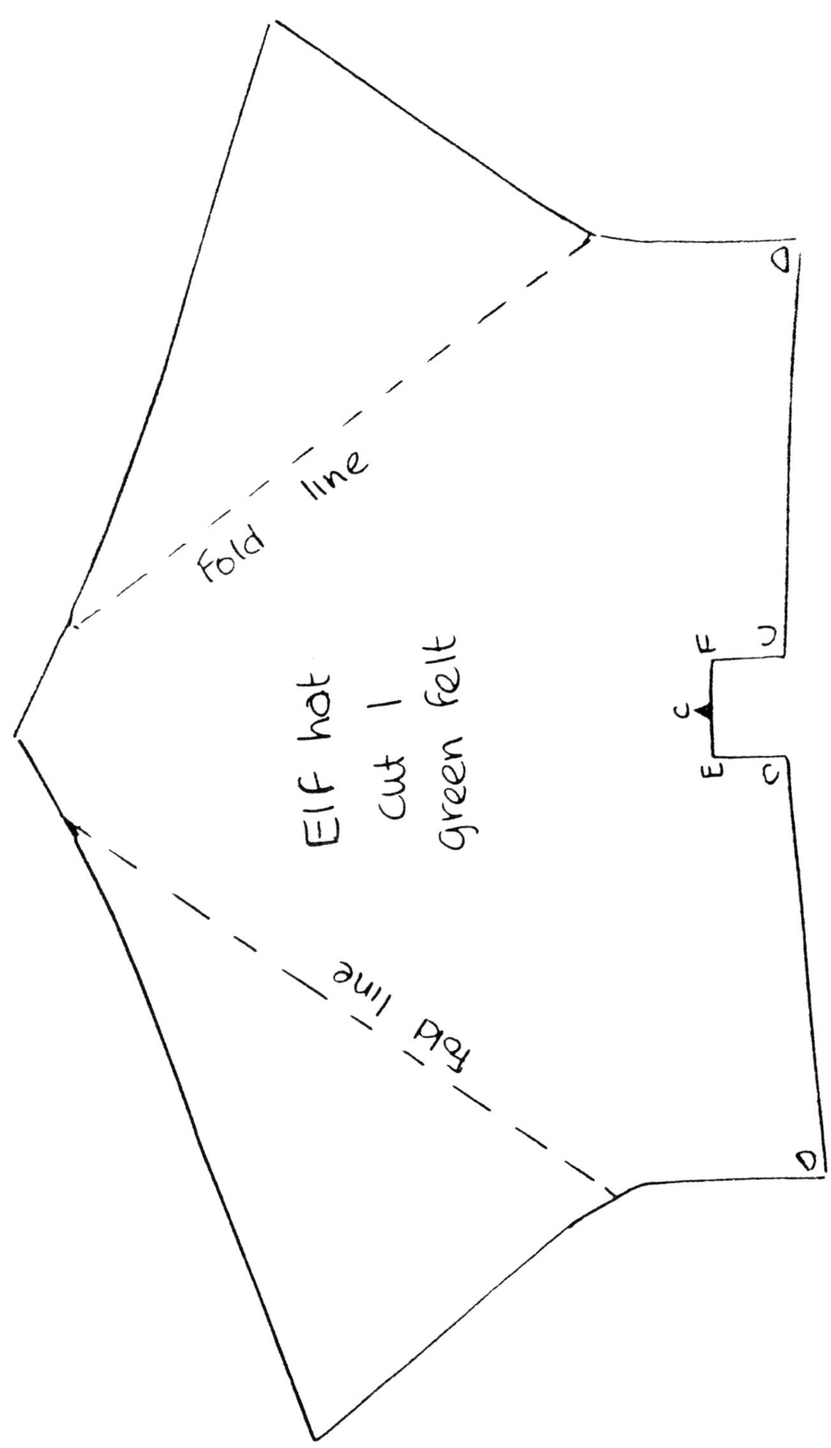

Illus. 38. Hat pattern for the Elf

Dangerous Dan, Desperado

Illus. 39

Materials: 25″ × 10″ blue gingham fabric, ⅛″ squares
iron-on interfacing for shirt
8″ × 8″ square red-and-white bandana fabric
6″ × 11″ brown medium-pile fur fabric
6″ × 9″ pink felt
5″ × 9″ blue denim
scraps of tan felt and silver lamé fabric
1 pair of plastic moving eyes, 12mm
cowboy-style hat
polyester fibre stuffing

BODY: Before making the body, stitch the pink hands to the ends of the arms along A-B. On the body front, glue the tan felt strip for the belt across the middle. Glue the buckle in position. Interface the shirt piece with medium-weight interfacing, and stitch it to the lower body (jeans). Topstitch where marked on the pattern to make the mock pockets and the fly on the jeans front. Now make the body according to the basic instructions on page 23.

HEAD: Place the hair in position on the head front. Secure the hair by topstitching all around it, near the edge. Proceed with head as described in the basic instructions on page 23, and then secure it to the body.

FACE: Make the nose following the circle technique (refer to page 8). Glue and stitch it in position in the middle of the face. Glue the eyes in place to either side of and slightly above the nose. Then glue the eyebrows and the moustache in position.

BANDANA & HAT: Cut the square bandana in half diagonally and tie it around the neck. The bandana may also be worn down around the neck, as shown in the drawing, or pulled up over the nose for hold-ups. Glue the hat (not shown) in position on the head.

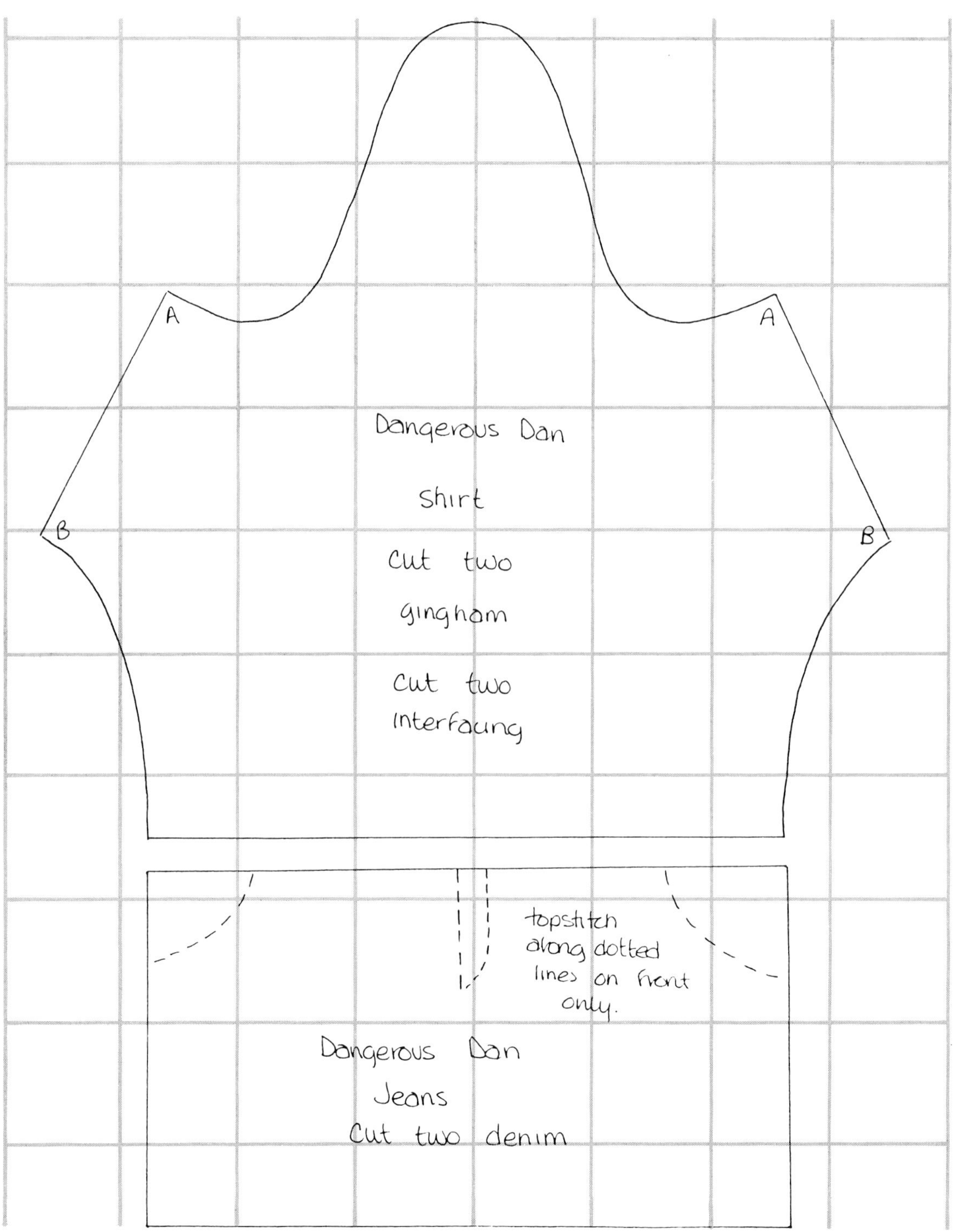

Illus. 40. Patterns for Dangerous Dan's shirt and jeans (75 percent of original size)

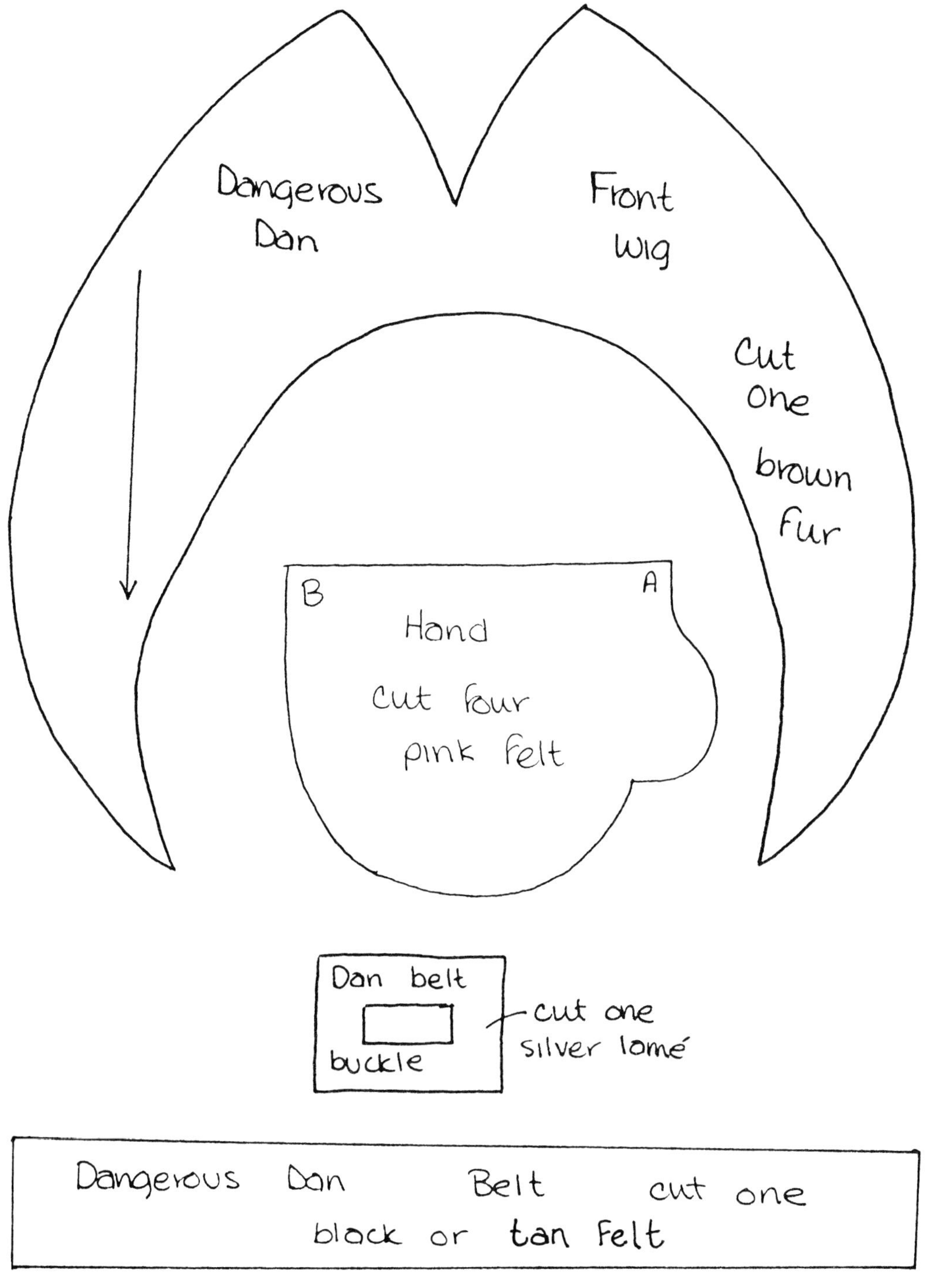

Illus. 41. Patterns for Dangerous Dan's hand, belt, belt buckle, and front wig

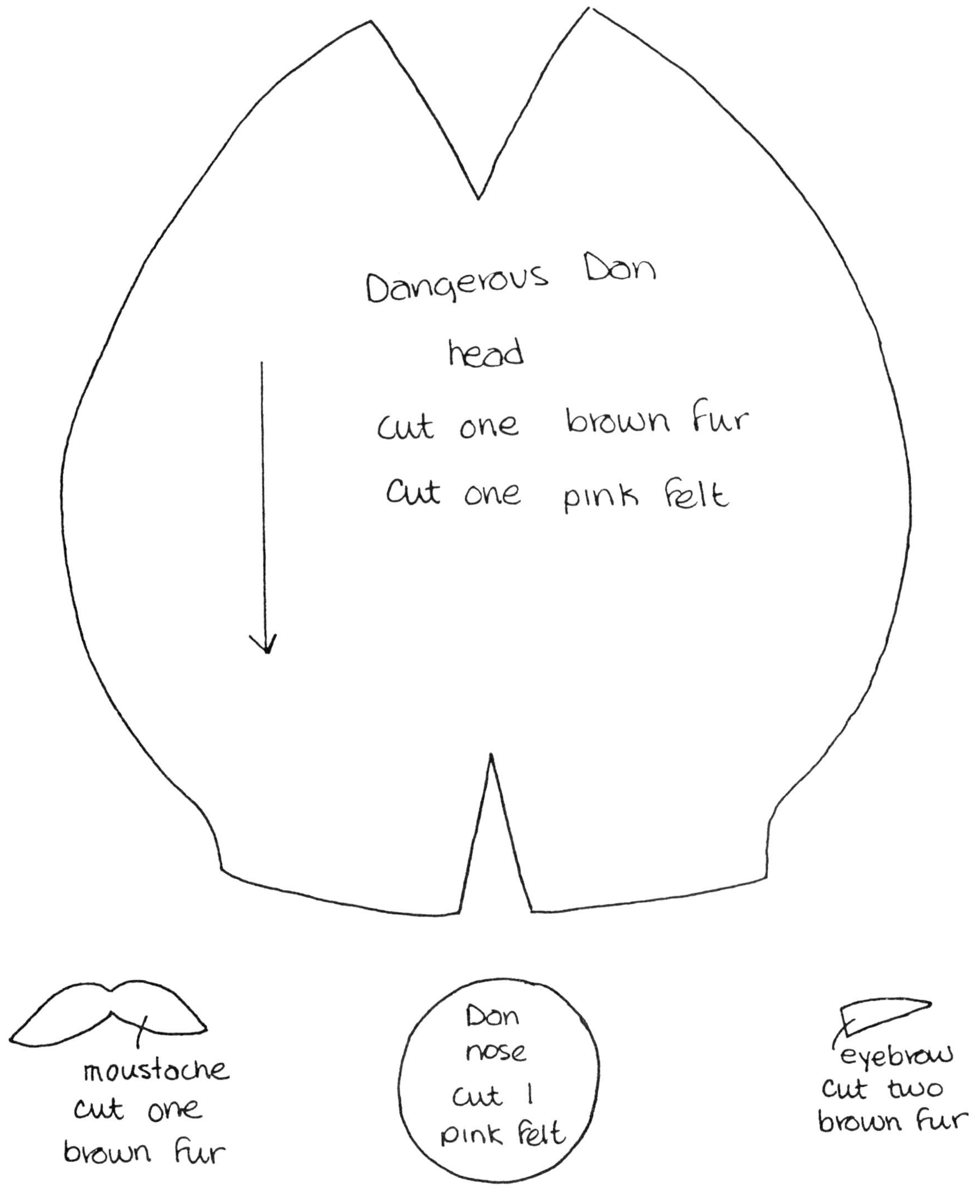

Illus. 42. Patterns for Dangerous Dan's head, moustache, nose, and eyebrow

Uriel Unicorn

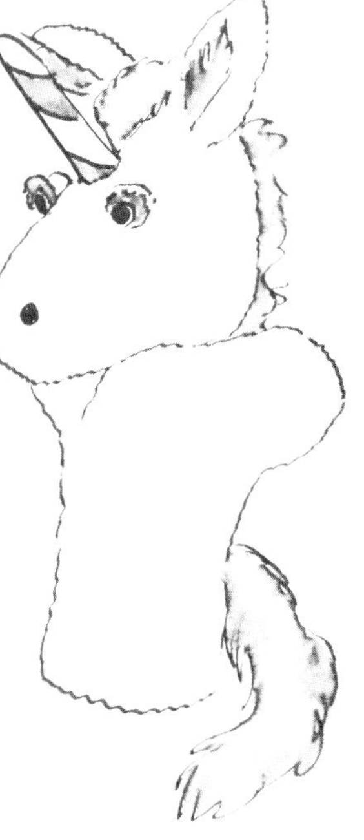

Illus. 43

Materials: 25″ × 13″ white fur fabric
10″ × 6″ long-pile pink fur fabric
small piece of gold lamé fabric
small pieces of pink, white, and black felt
polyester fibre stuffing

TAIL: Fold the tail in half lengthwise, with the right sides facing, and stitch from the curved end along the long edge, leaving the end open. Turn right side out.

BODY: Make the body following the basic instructions on page 23. Make a small slit in the body back, and poke the raw end of the tail through from the right side. Then stitch the slit closed, catching the tail in your stitching.

EARS: Stitch the ears, with their right sides facing, together in pairs. Turn right side out. Glue the ear lining in place on the front of the ear and then topstitch all around the edge, through all the layers.

HORN: Stitch the gold lamé horn to the pink felt horn along the curve between X and Y, with the right sides facing and matching the X of one piece to the Y of the other. (Do not match X to X or Y to Y because the horn will spiral only if it's properly stitched.) Folding the horn pieces so that the edges meet, stitch each side from X/Y to Z. Turn the horn right side out. If properly stitched, the horn should spiral.

FACE & HEAD: Stitch darts in the sides of the head, with the right sides facing. Next, stitch the head pieces together all around the edge, with the right sides facing and leaving the straight neck edge open along A-B. Turn the head right side out and then stuff it following the basic instructions on page 24. Attach it to the body as described. Now stitch the ears and horn in place, referring to the drawing for positioning.

EYES & NOSE: Fold the pink eyelash pieces in half lengthwise, with their wrong sides facing. Catching the lower edge of the eyelids in between, topstitch along the edge of the eyelash so that the edge of the eyelid is bound. Trim the eyelashes with scissors. Make the eyeballs using the circle technique (refer to page 8). Glue the black pupils to the eyeballs. Apply the lids to the eyes, stitching in position. Glue and stitch the eyeballs in position on the head. Then glue the nostrils to the front of the face.

Illus. 44. Patterns for Uriel Unicorn's ear, ear lining, and horn

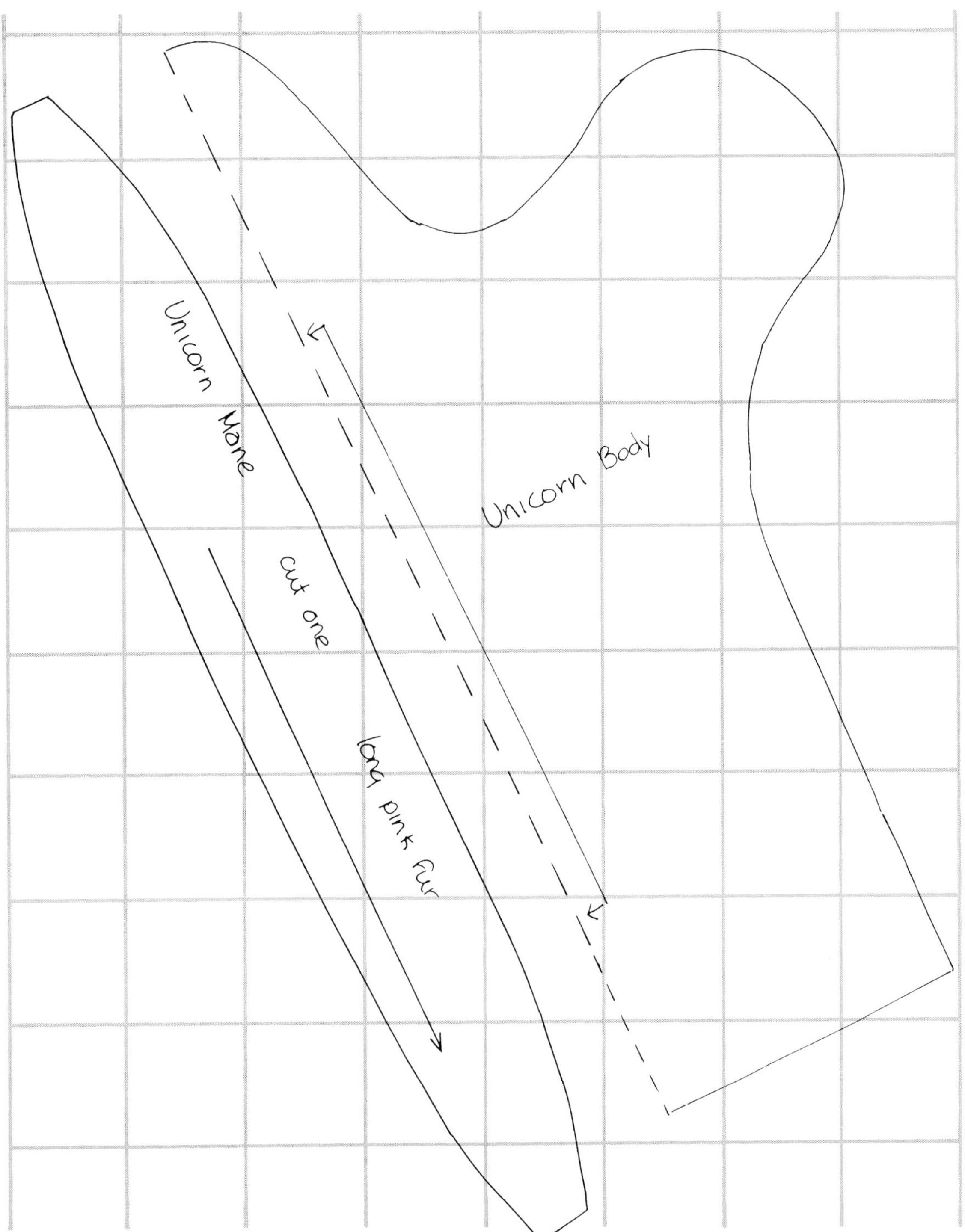

Illus. 45. Patterns for Uriel Unicorn's body and mane (75 percent of their original size)

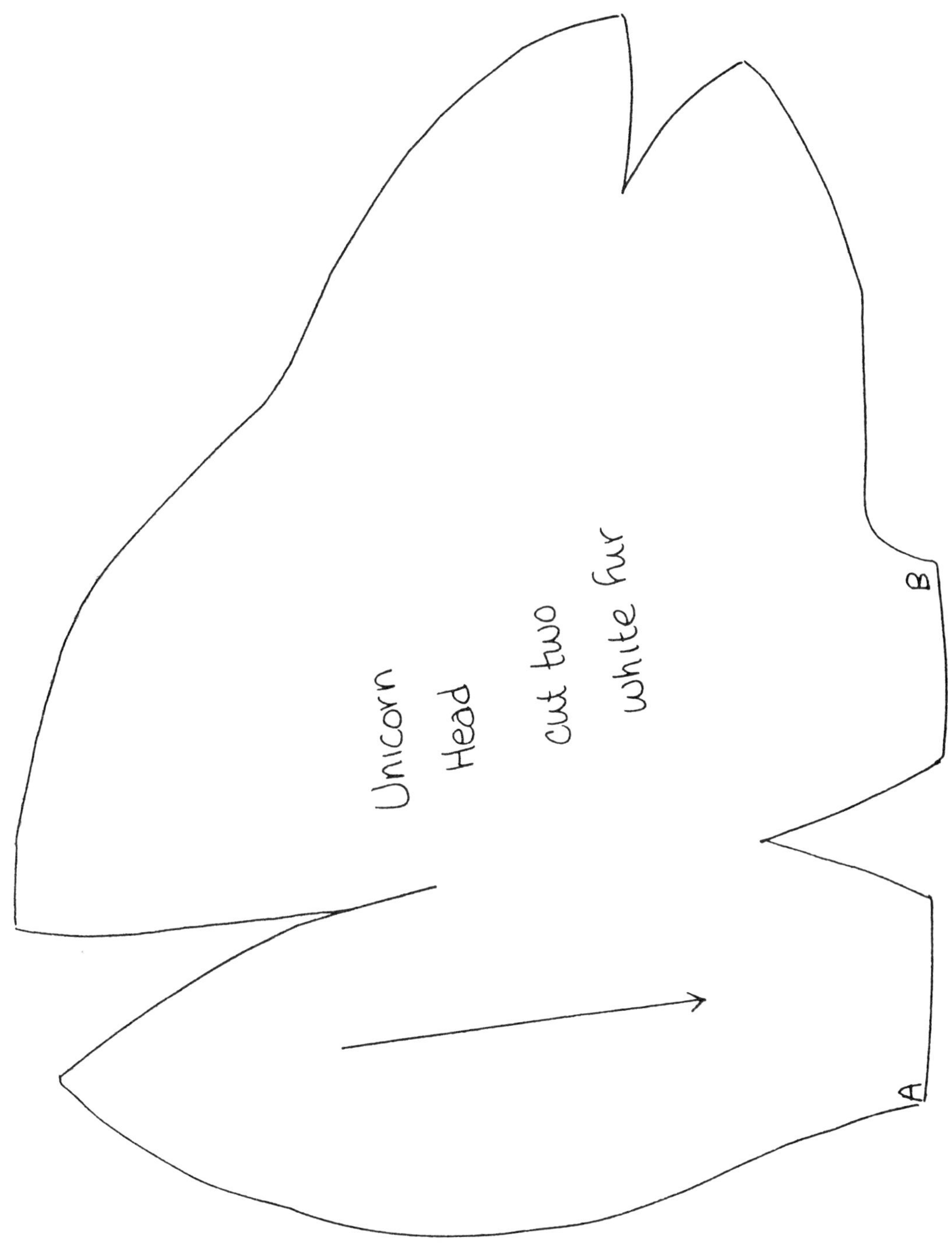

Illus. 46. Head pattern for Uriel Unicorn

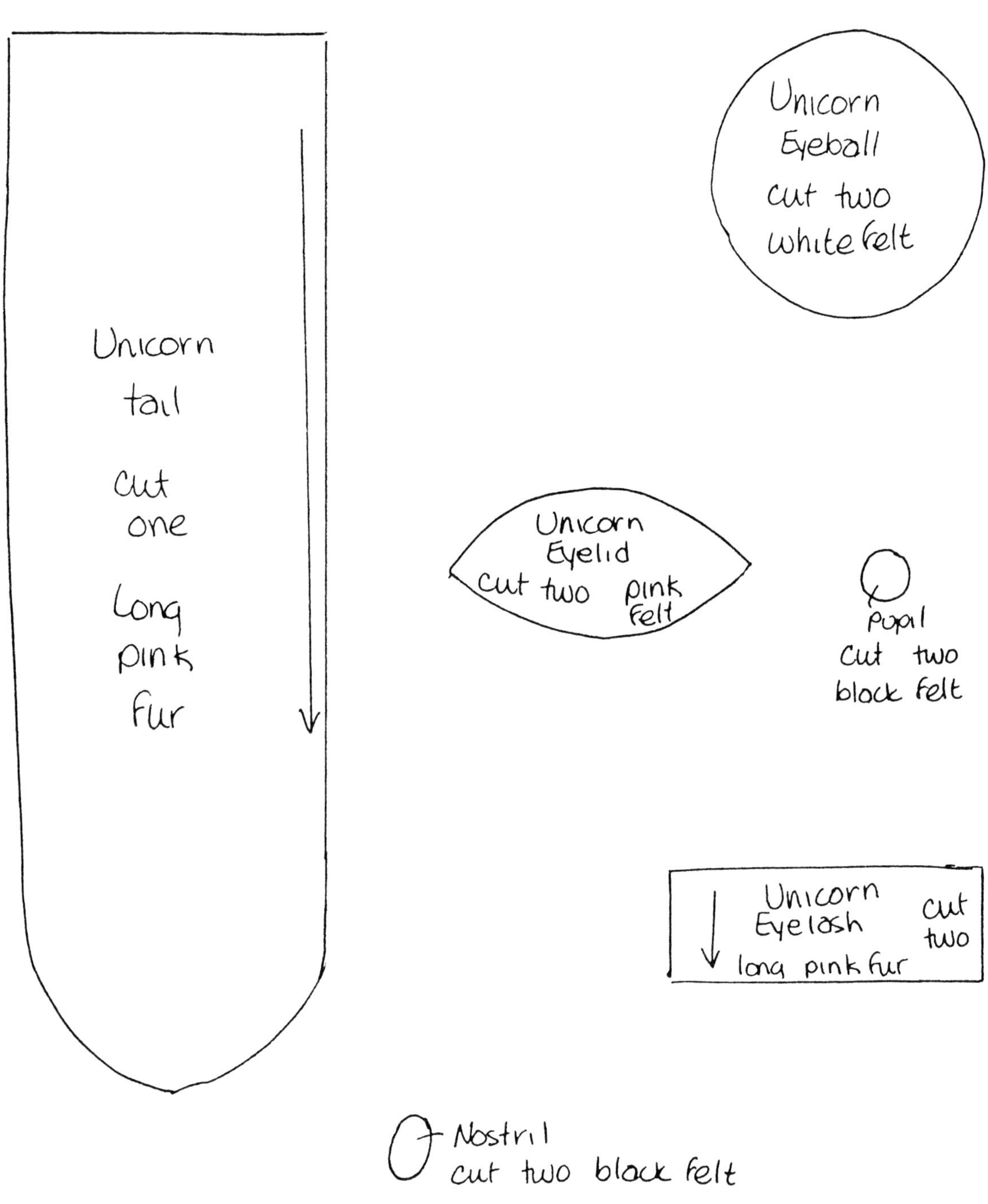

Illus. 47. Patterns for Uriel Unicorn's tail, eyes, and nostrils

Christmas Reindeer

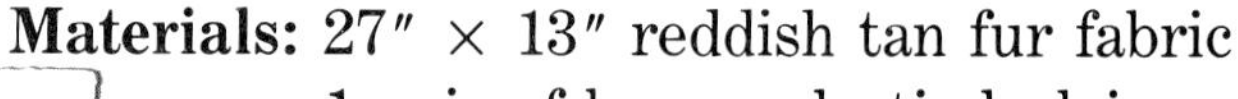

Illus. 48

Materials: 27″ × 13″ reddish tan fur fabric
1 pair of brown plastic lock-in eyes, 15mm
4″ × 12″ brown felt
scraps of white fur
scrap of red felt
polyester fibre stuffing

BODY: Make the body, following the basic instructions on page 23.

EARS: Stitch the ears together in pairs, with the right sides facing. Turn them right side out. Glue the ear lining in place on the front of the ear and then topstitch all around the edge, through all the layers.

HEAD: Stitch darts in the sides of the head, with the right sides facing. Next, stitch the head pieces together along A-B, with the right sides facing. Matching notch A on the head gusset to point A on the head pieces, stitch the head gusset to the head. Make small holes for the eyes where indicated on the pattern. Turn the head right side out and apply safety eyes by pushing the stems through the holes and fastening them from the back with lock washers. Stuff the head as described in the basic instructions on page 24; then attach it to the body as described.

ANTLERS: Stitch the antlers together in pairs, with the right sides facing and near the edge, leaving the bottom straight edge open. Stuff the antlers carefully and then stitch them to the top of the head, following the drawing for positioning.

NOSE & FACE: Make the nose using the circle technique (refer to page 8); then stitch and glue it in position on the front of the snout. Then stitch the ears to the head, following the drawing for positioning.

TAIL: Stitch together in pairs, with the right sides facing, along C-D. Matching points C and E, stitch the tail gusset to the tail, leaving an opening between D and E. Turn the tail right side out and stuff it firmly. Then stitch it to the lower body back.

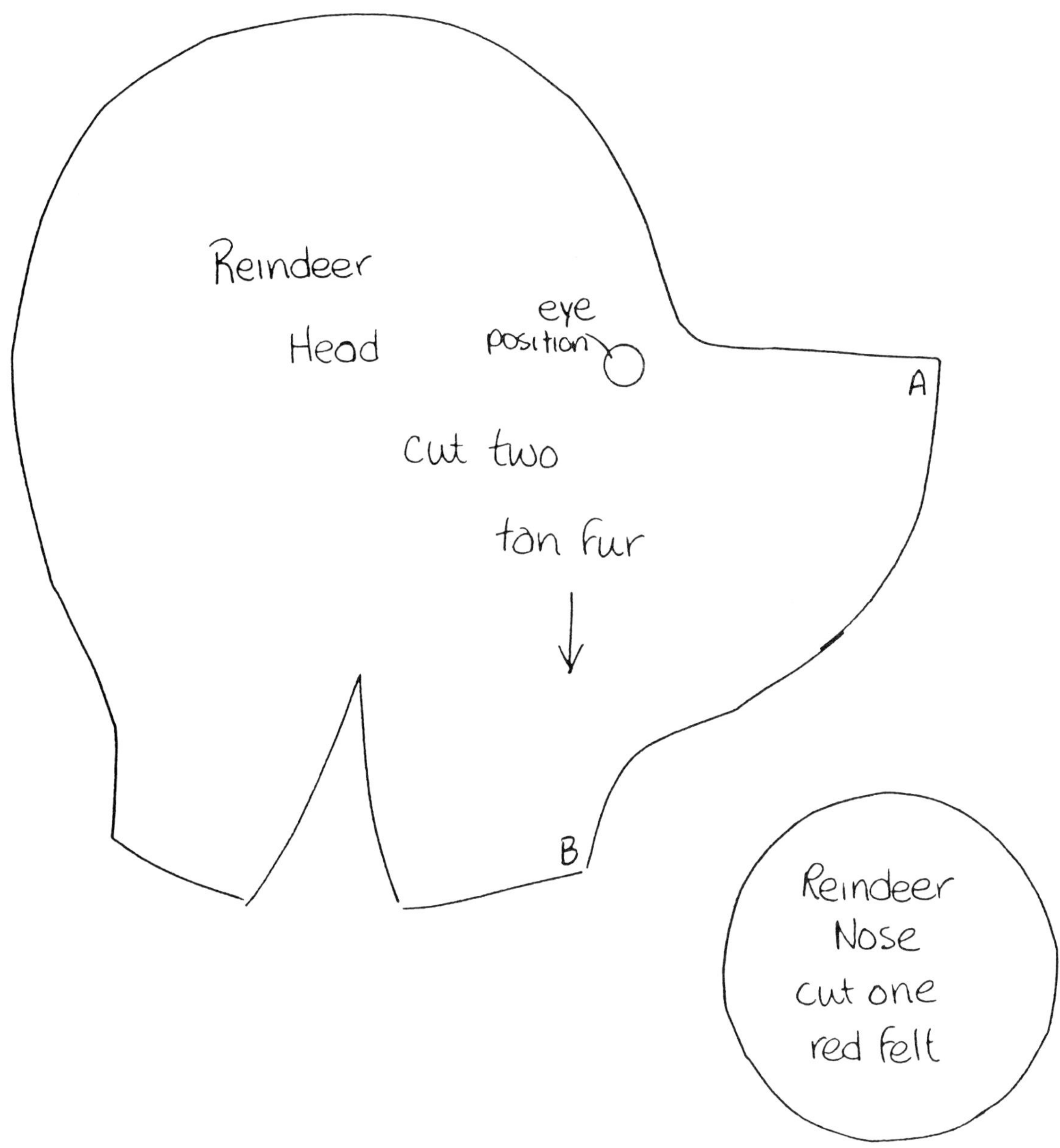

Illus 49. Head and nose patterns for Christmas Reindeer

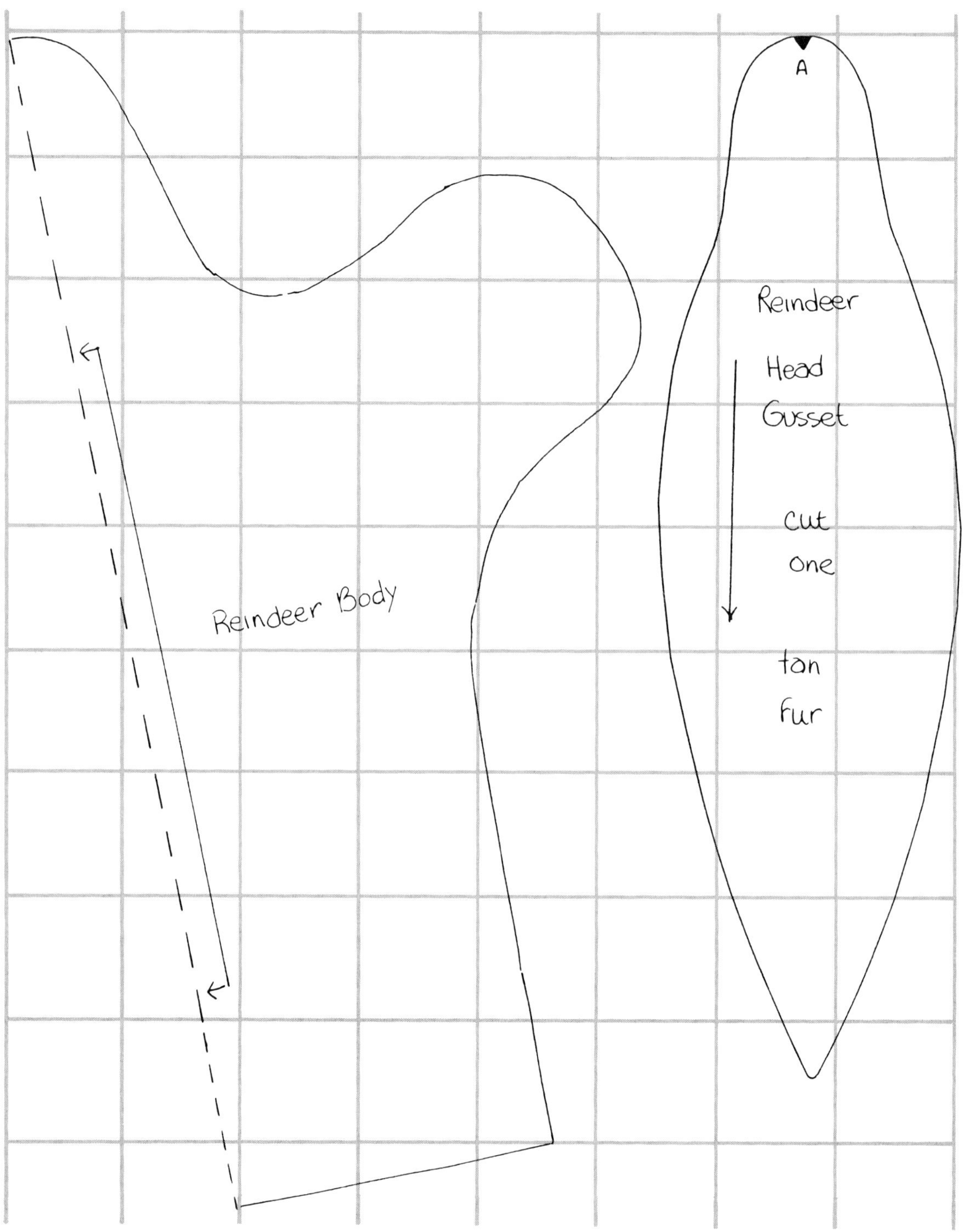

Illus. 50. Body and head-gusset patterns for Christmas Reindeer (75 percent of their original size)

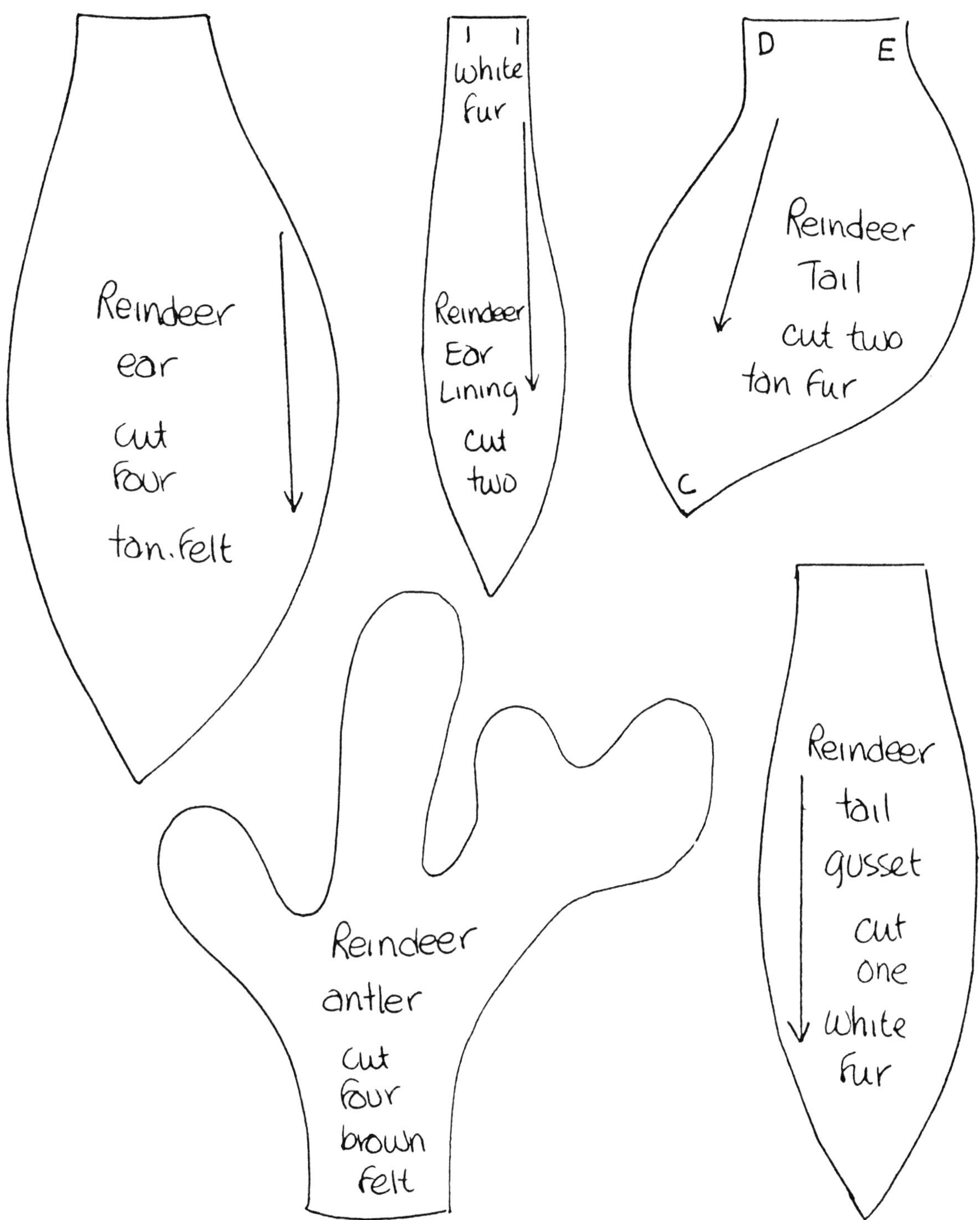

Illus. 51. Ear, ear lining, tail, tail gusset, and antler patterns for Christmas Reindeer

Terence the Terrible Troll

Illus. 52

Materials: 25″ × 13″ tan burlap or other firm coarsely woven fabric
6″ × 11″ brown medium-pile fur fabric
6″ × 12″ tan felt
scraps of yellow, black, and hot-pink felt
scrap of silver lamé fabric
1 pair of plastic moving eyes, 12mm
red thread
polyester fibre stuffing

BODY: Before making the body, stitch the tan hands to the ends of the arms along A-B. On the body front, glue the brown felt strip for the belt across the middle. Glue the silver lamé buckle in position. Now make the body, following the basic instructions on page 23.

EARS: Stitch the ears together in pairs, with the right sides facing, leaving the straight edge open. Turn the ears right side out and finger-press them flat. Set them aside.

HEAD: Place the face in position on the head front. Secure it by topstitching all around and close to the edge. Matching raw edges, baste the ears in position on the side of the head. Now proceed with the head, as described in the basic instructions on page 23, and then secure it to the body.

FACE: Make a crooked mouth with red thread by embroidering it in position. Make the nose, following the circle technique on page 8. Gather it up into an oval, and take two tight stitches to form nostrils along one edge. Glue and stitch the nose in position in the middle of the face. Glue the eyes in place to either side of and slightly above the nose.

Whimsical Wilhelm, Wizard

Illus. 53

Materials: 25″ × 13″ black velveteen
6″ × 11″ silver-grey long-pile fur fabric
6″ × 12″ pink felt
5″ × 5″ black felt
scrap of hot-pink felt
scraps of gold and silver lamé fabric
1 pair of plastic moving eyes, 12mm
polyester fibre stuffing

BODY: Before making the body, stitch the pink hands to the ends of the arms along A-B. Now make the body, following the basic instructions on page 23.

HEAD: Place the face in position on the head front. Secure it by topstitching all around and close to the edge. Proceed with the head, as described in the basic instructions on page 23, and then secure it to the body.

FACE: Make the nose, following the circle technique on page 8. Glue and stitch it in position in the middle of the face. Glue the eyes in place to either side of and just above the nose.

HAT: Fold the hat, with the right sides facing, so that the straight edges meet. Stitch along the straight edge from the wide end to the point, forming a cone. Turn right side out and stuff, following the directions on page 7. Glue and stitch the hat to the Wizard's head.

SPANGLES: Glue a crescent moon to the hat and shirt. Sprinkle gold and silver lamé stars randomly over the hat and shirt; then glue them in place.

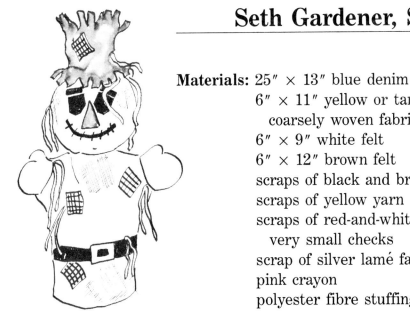

Illus. 54

Seth Gardener, Scarecrow

Materials: 25″ × 13″ blue denim
6″ × 11″ yellow or tan burlap or coarsely woven fabric
6″ × 9″ white felt
6″ × 12″ brown felt
scraps of black and brown felt
scraps of yellow yarn
scraps of red-and-white gingham with very small checks
scrap of silver lamé fabric
pink crayon
polyester fibre stuffing

BODY: Before making the body, stitch the white hands to the ends of the arms along A-B. On the body front, glue the brown felt strip for the belt across the middle. Glue the silver lamé buckle in position. Now make the body, as described in the basic instructions on page 23.

HEAD: Proceed with the head, as described in the basic instructions on page 23 and then secure it to the body.

FACE: Glue the eyes, mouth, and nose in position on the face. Color the cheeks slightly with pink crayon.

HAT: Fold the upper-hat piece, with the right sides facing, so that the short edges meet; then stitch them together along the short edge to form a tube. Stitch the upper hat to the brim along the inner-circle edge. Cut the edges of the hat jaggedly and snip small holes in the hat. Attach the hat to the head with small stitches and a dab of glue.

PATCHES & STRAW: Create the straw effect by making loose stitches with yellow yarn in a large needle. Tie the ends together and leave about ¾ inch hanging. Glue patches cut from gingham randomly over the denim body and hat.

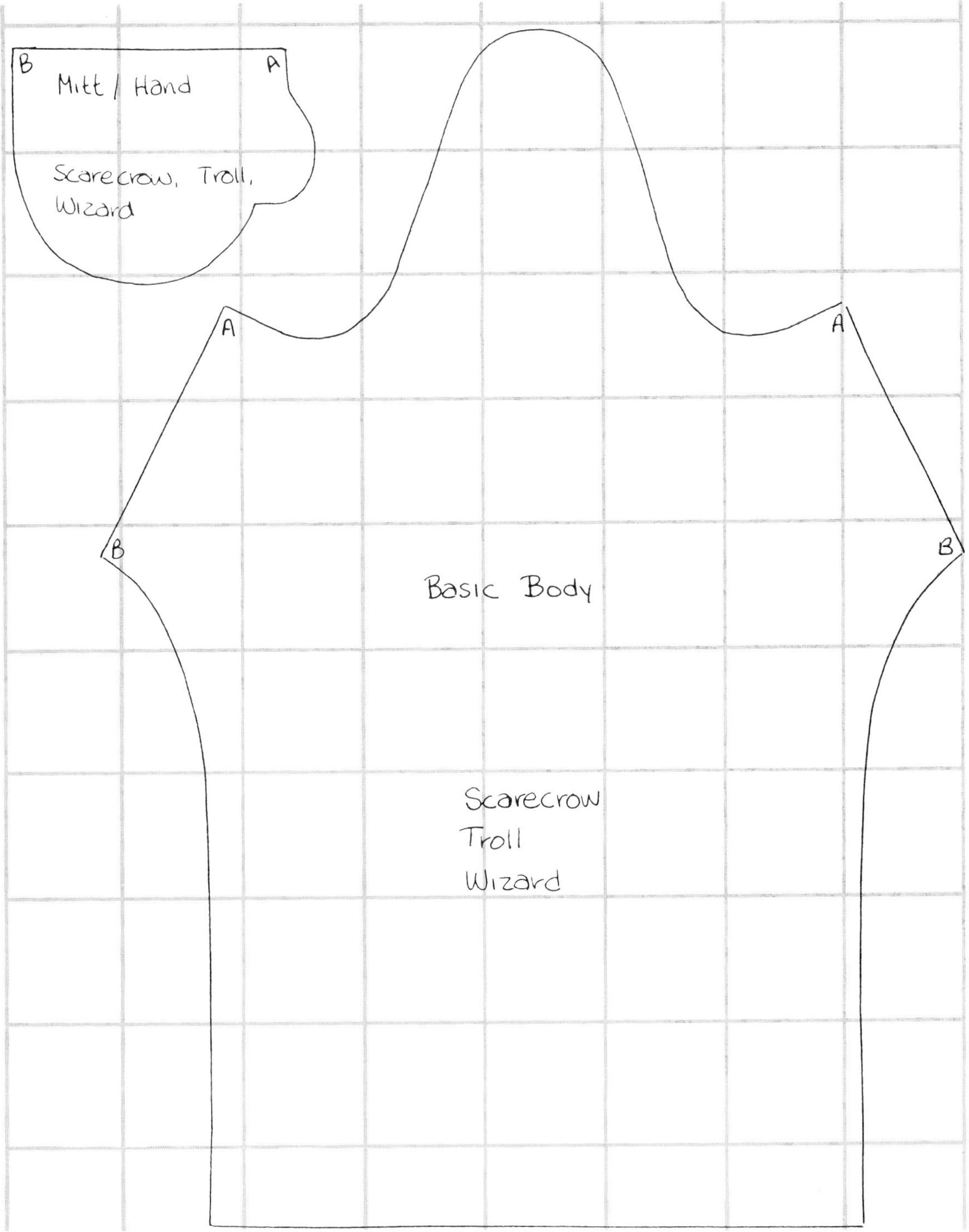

Illus. 55. Basic body and mitt, or hand, patterns for the Scarecrow, Troll, and Wizard (75 percent of their original size)

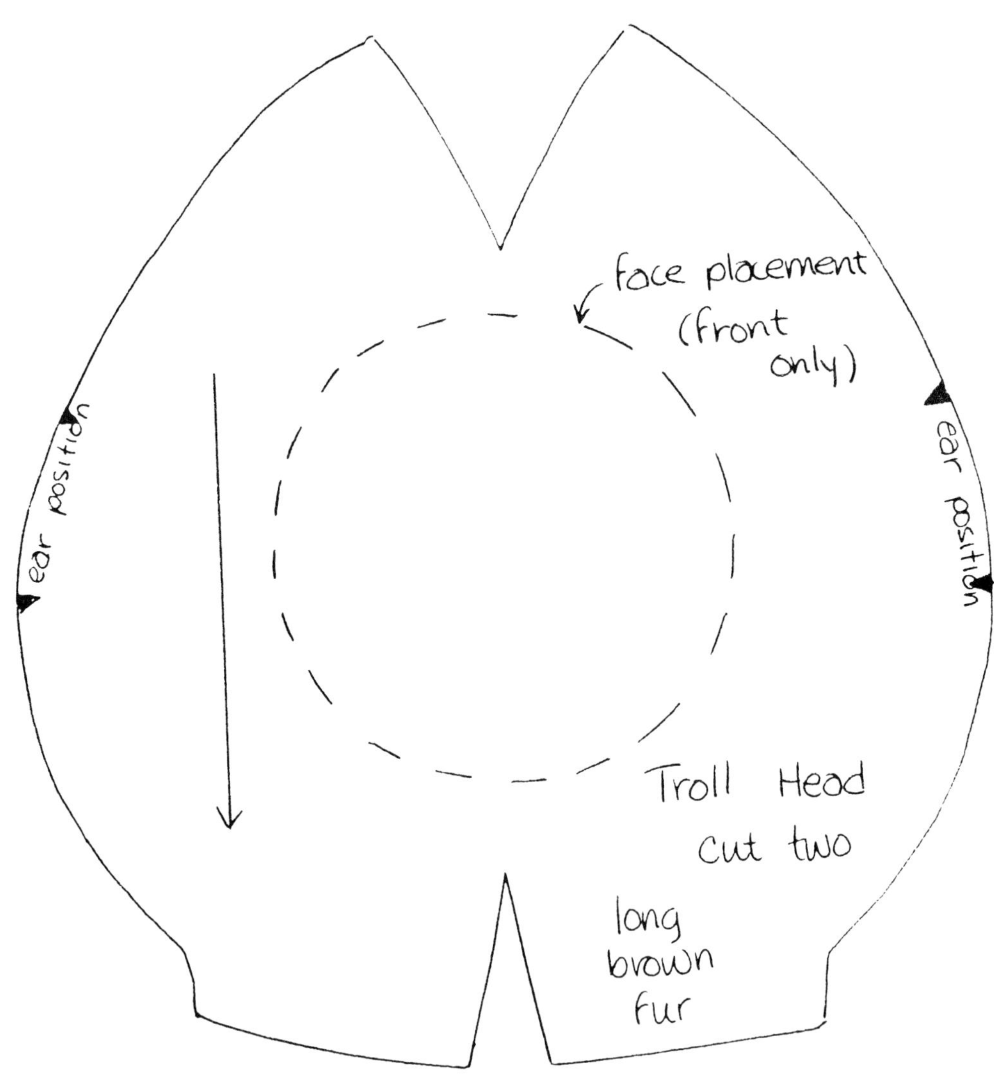

Illus. 56. Head pattern for Terence the Terrible Troll

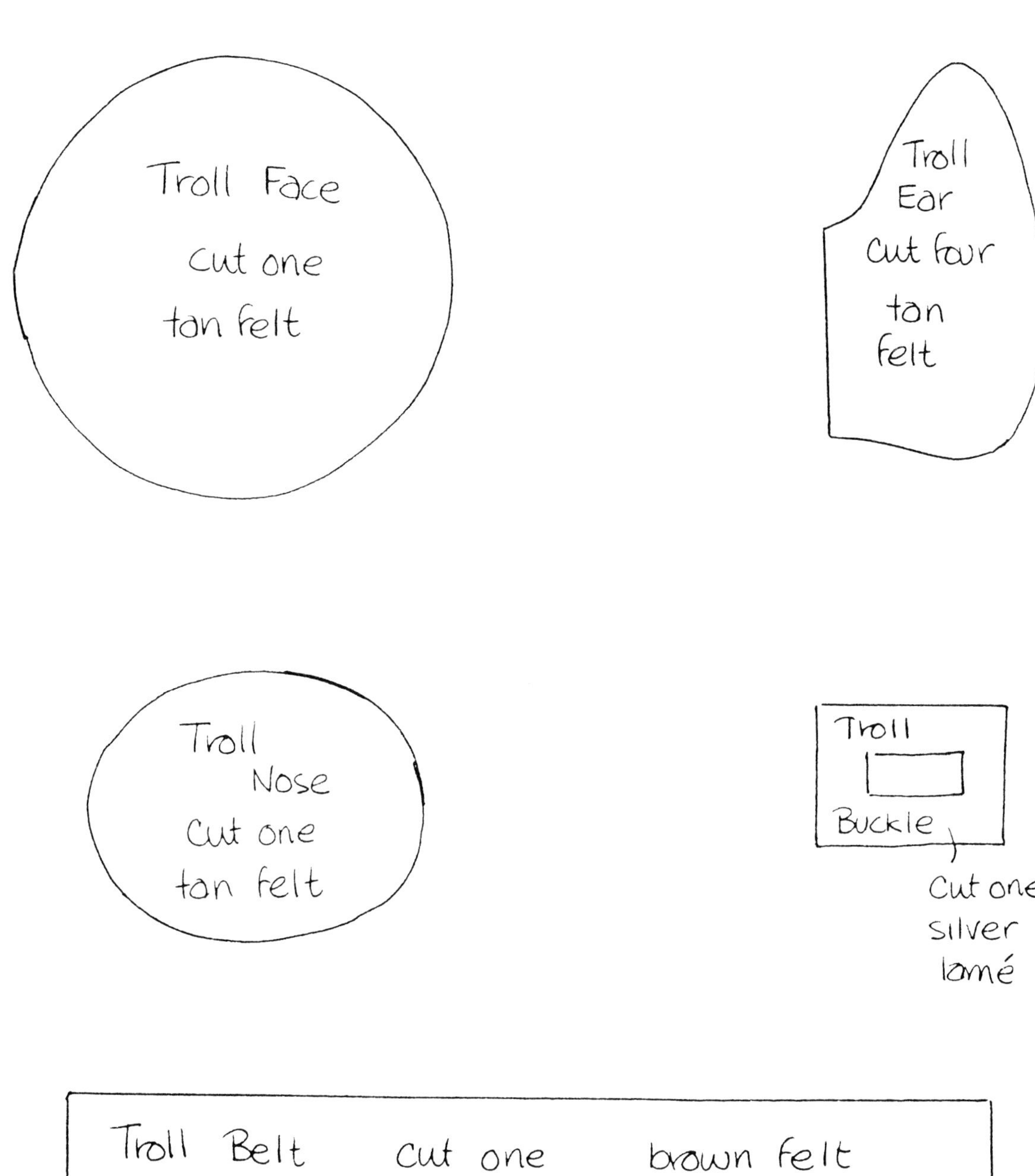

Illus. 57. Additional patterns for the Troll

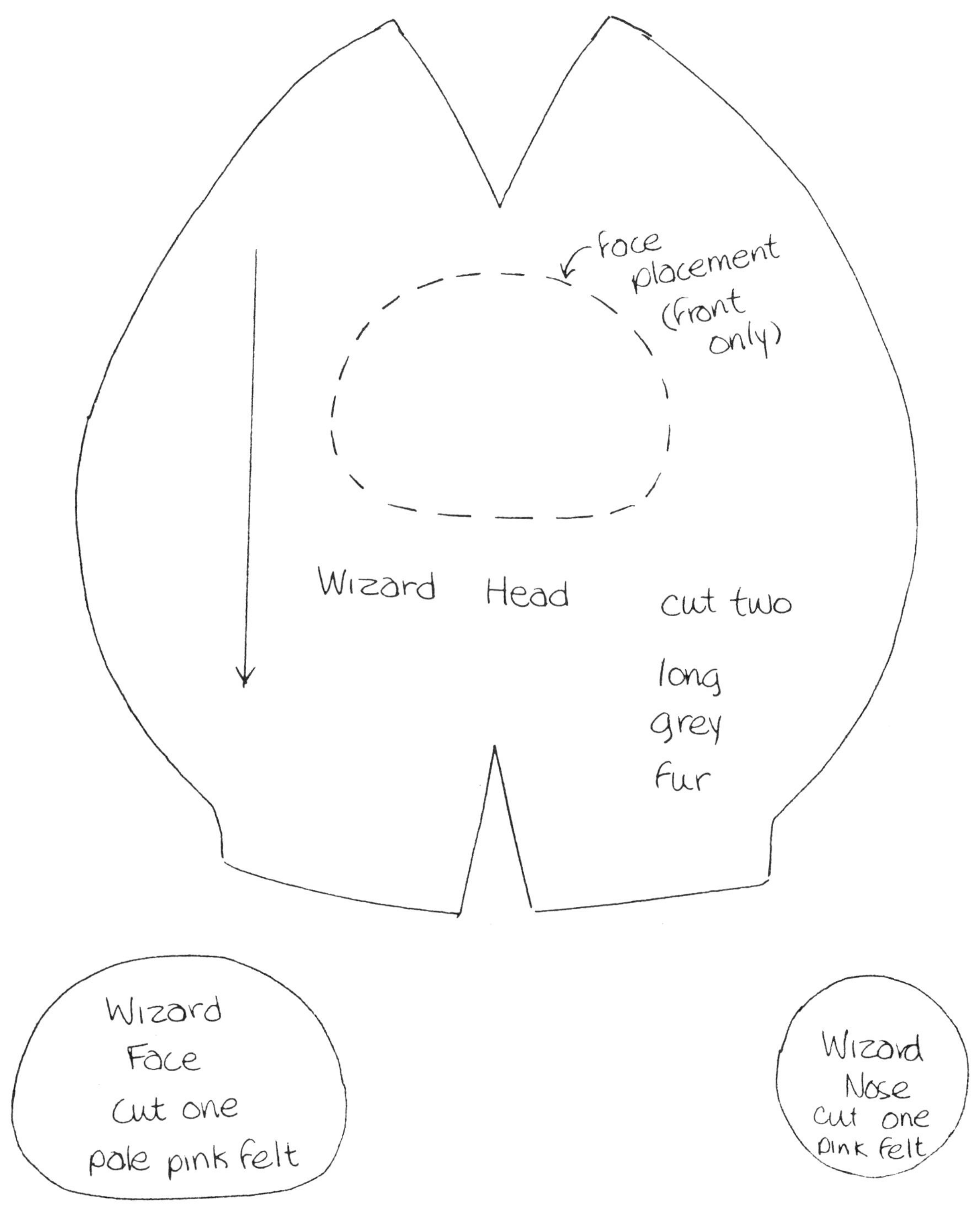

Illus. 58. Head, face, and nose patterns for Whimsical Wilhelm Wizard

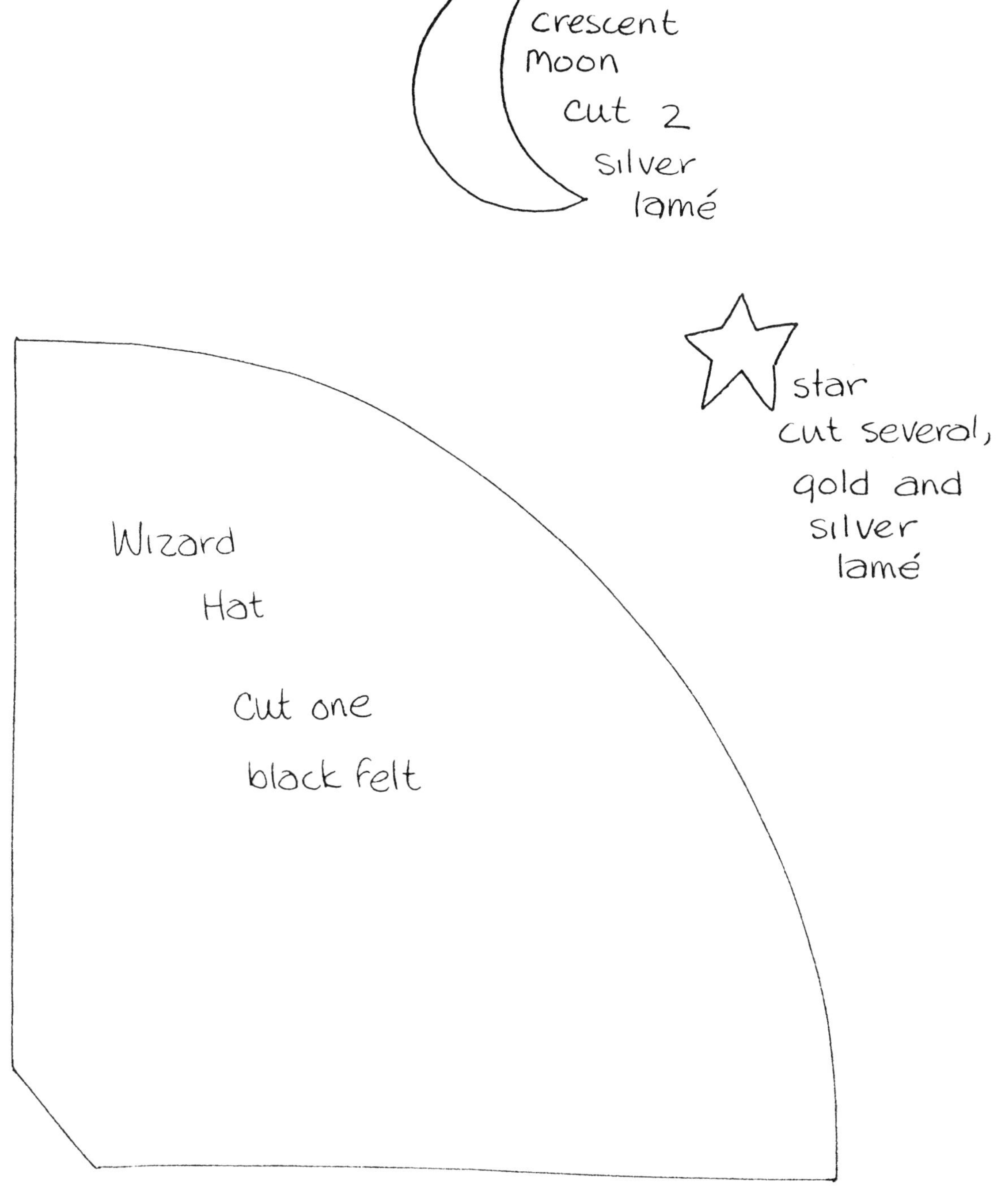

Illus. 59. Additional patterns for the Wizard

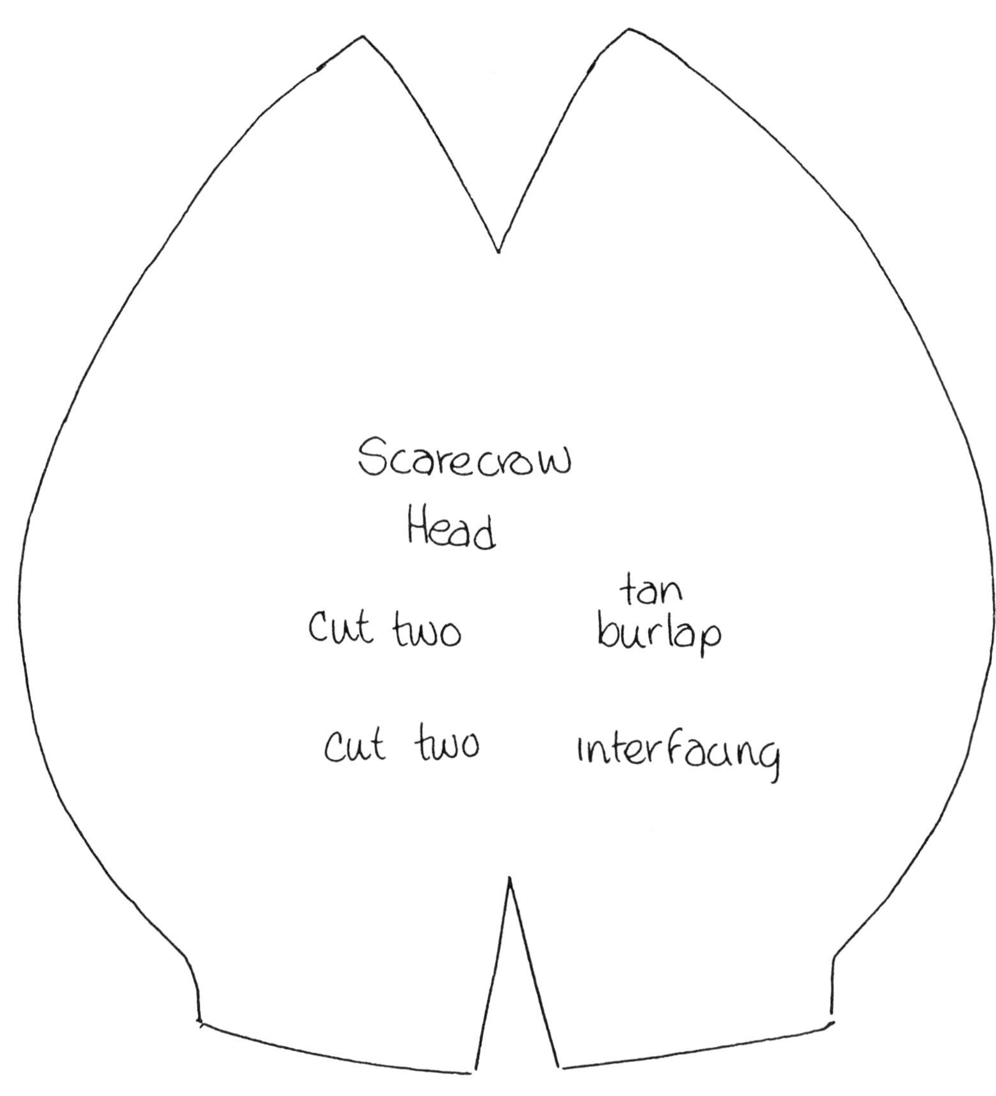

Basic Body: denim
Hands: white felt

Illus. 60. Head pattern for Seth Gardener, Scarecrow, and note regarding material for his basic body and hands

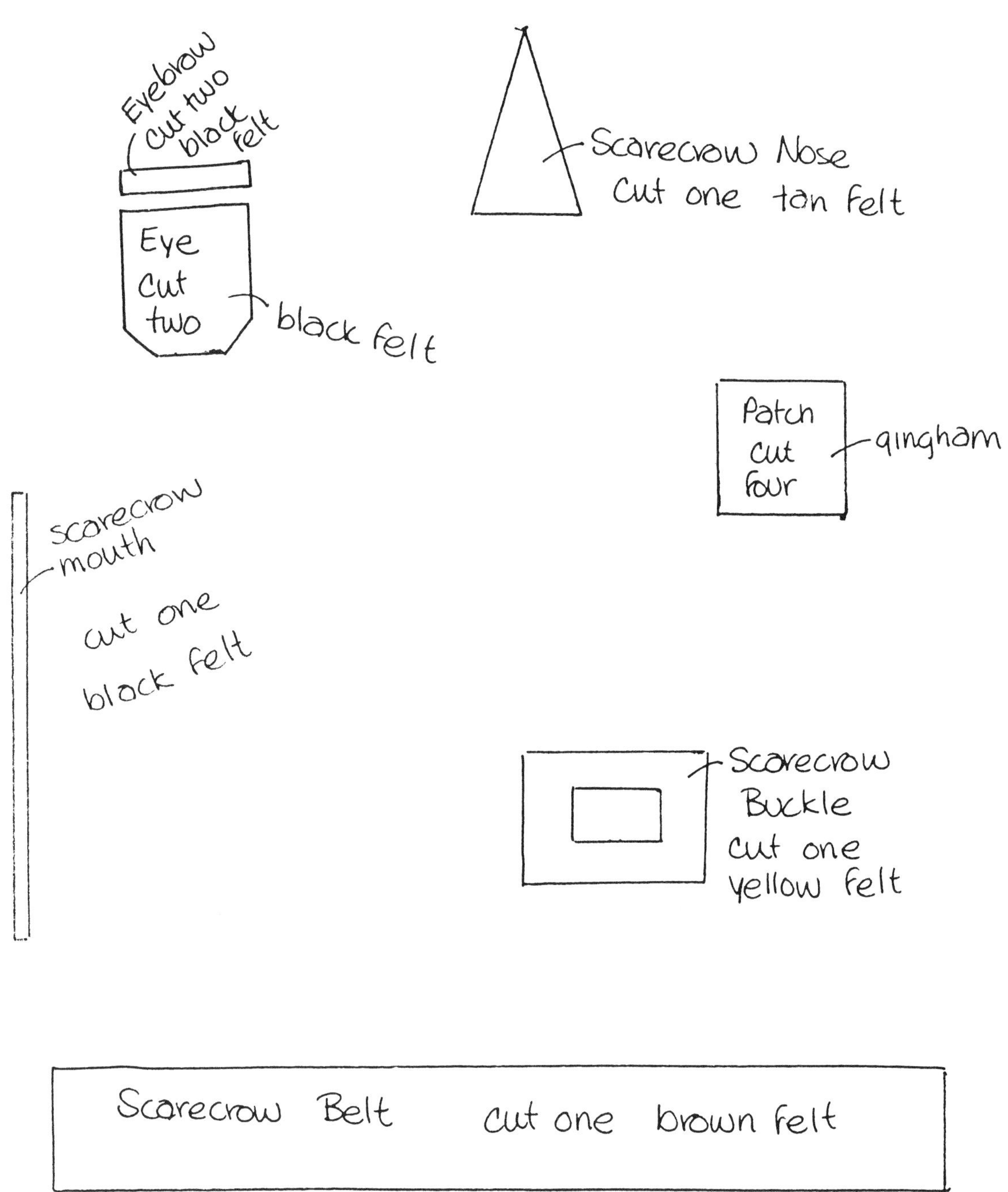

Illus. 61. Patterns for the Scarecrow's mouth, nose, eyes, eyebrows, patch, buckle, and belt

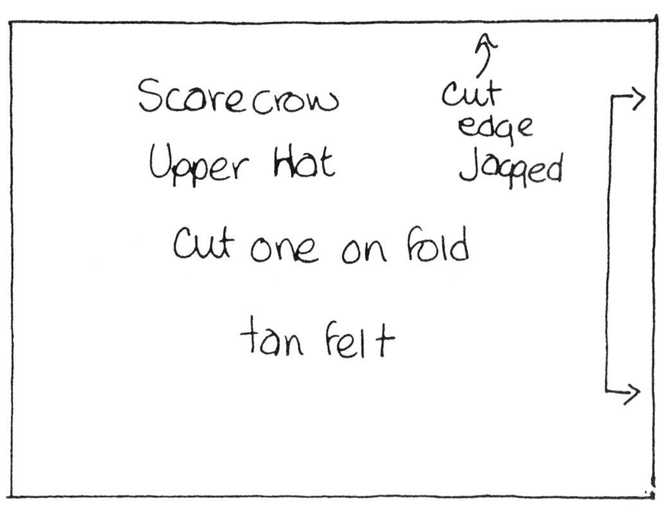

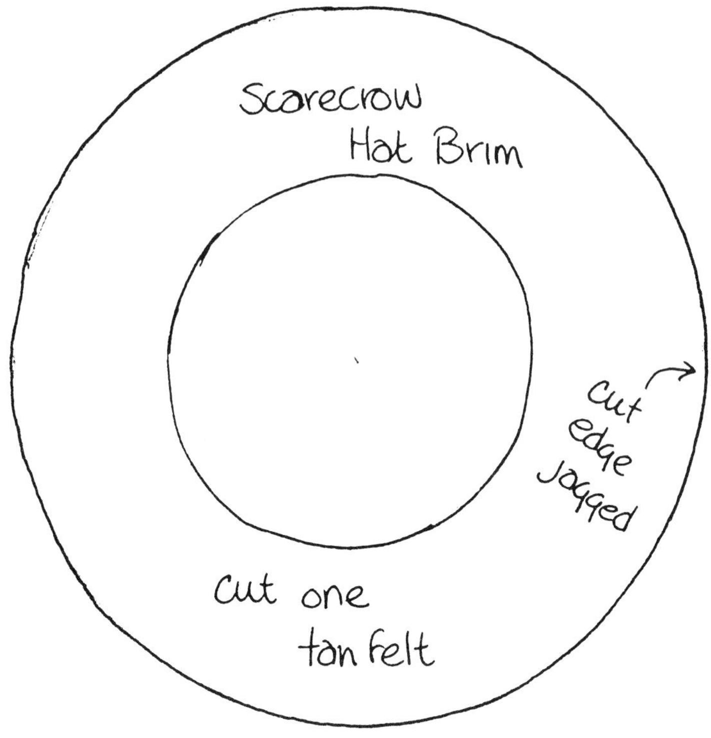

Illus. 62. Patterns for the Scarecrow's hat

Kristabel Kangaroo and Baby

Illus. 63

Materials: 27″ × 13″ light-tan fur fabric
1 pair of brown plastic lock-in eyes, 12mm
¼″ piece of elastic, 3″ long
scraps of black felt
polyester fibre stuffing

BODY: Fold ⅜ inch along the top edge of the pouch to the wrong side and stitch it in place to make a hem and the channel for the elastic. Run the elastic through, taking a stitch at either end to secure it. Turn under the curved edge of the pouch and stitch it in place on the body front, with the wrong side of the pouch facing the right side of the body front. Continue making the body, following the basic instructions on page 23.

EARS: Stitch the ears together in pairs, with the right sides facing. Turn right side out.

HEAD: Stitch darts in the head sides with the right sides facing. Stitch the head pieces together, with the right sides facing, along A-B. Fold the ears in half lengthwise, and baste them, facing forward, in position on the sides of the head. Matching notch A on the head gusset to point A on the head pieces, stitch the head gusset to the head, catching the ears in your stitching. Make small holes for the eyes where indicated on the pattern. Turn the head right side out and apply safety eyes by pushing the stems through the holes and fastening them from the back with lock washers. Stuff, according to the basic instructions on page 24. Attach the head to the body, as described in the basic instructions.

BABY: Stitch the baby body, with the right sides facing, along C-D. Make the ears as described for the mother. Baste the ears in place along the right edge of the body back. With the right sides facing and matching points C, stitch the body front to the body back, leaving the bottom open. Turn right side out and glue the nose and eyes in position. Tuck the baby kangaroo into the mother's pouch.

Ashley Ape

Illus. 64

Materials: 22″ × 16″ grey fur fabric
5″ × 8″ medium-pile white fur
4″ × 6″ tan felt
1 pair of brown plastic lock-in eyes, 12mm
1 small plastic animal nose
polyester fibre stuffing

BODY: Place the stomach piece in position on the body front, with the wrong side of the stomach facing the right side of the body front. Topstitch all around and close to the edge. Make up the body, as described in the basic instructions on page 23.

FACE: With the right sides facing, stitch darts in the snout pieces. With the right sides facing and matching A-B, stitch the top snout to the top face along A-B. With the right sides facing, stitch the lower snout to the top snout along A-C-A. Turn the face right side out and poke a tiny hole for the nose. Insert the nose and glue it securely in position. Stuff the lower snout piece and then topstitch the face in position on the head front.

HEAD: Before sewing the head, poke holes for the eyes where indicated on the pattern; then push the stems through the holes from the right side and fasten them from the back with lock washers. Fold the ears along the dotted line indicated on the pattern and then baste them in position, facing forward, on the head front. Finish the head, as described in the basic instructions on page 23, catching the ears in your stitching. Now attach the head to the body, as described in the basic instructions.

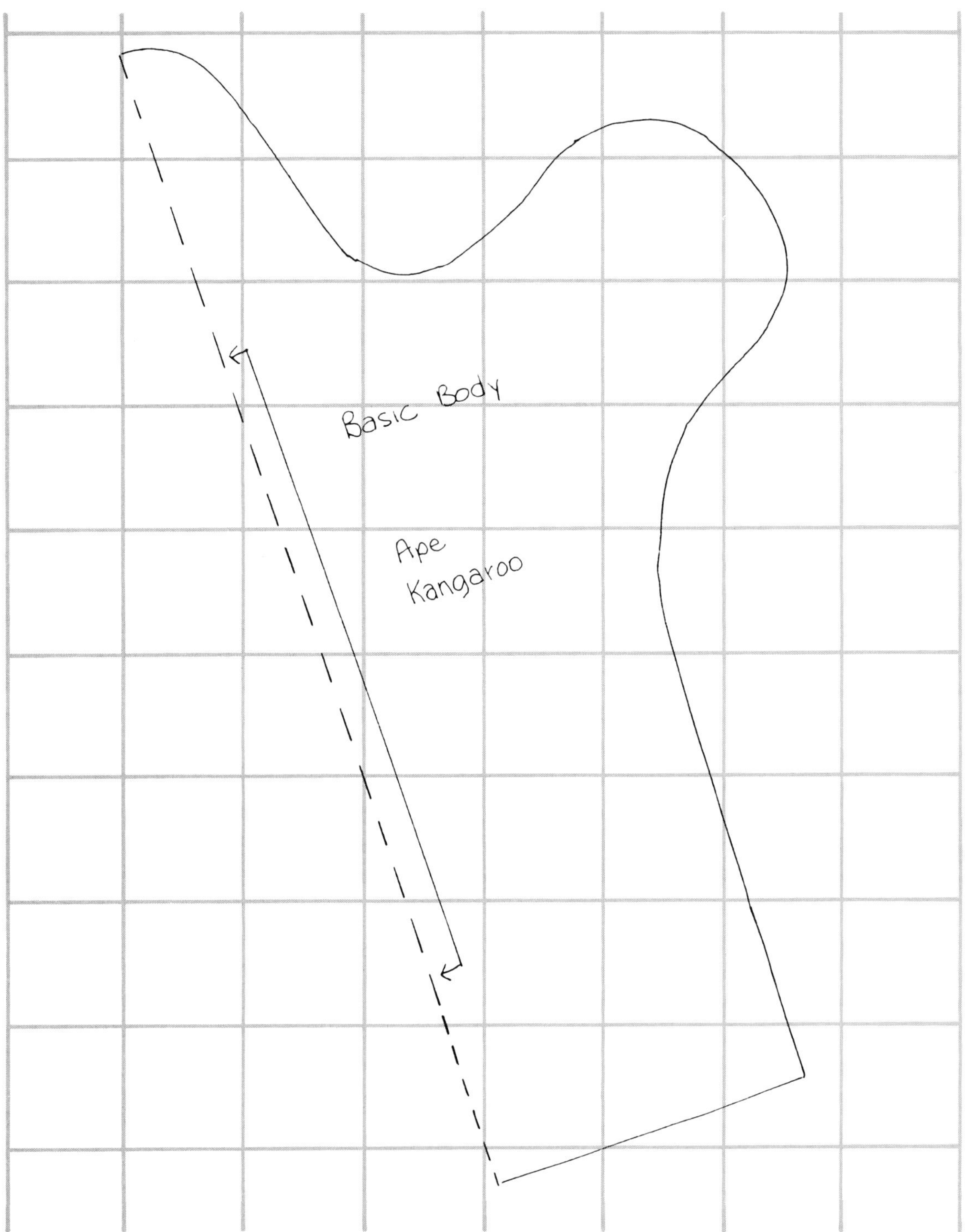

Illus. 65. Basic body for Kristabel Kangaroo and Ashley Ape (75 percent of its original size)

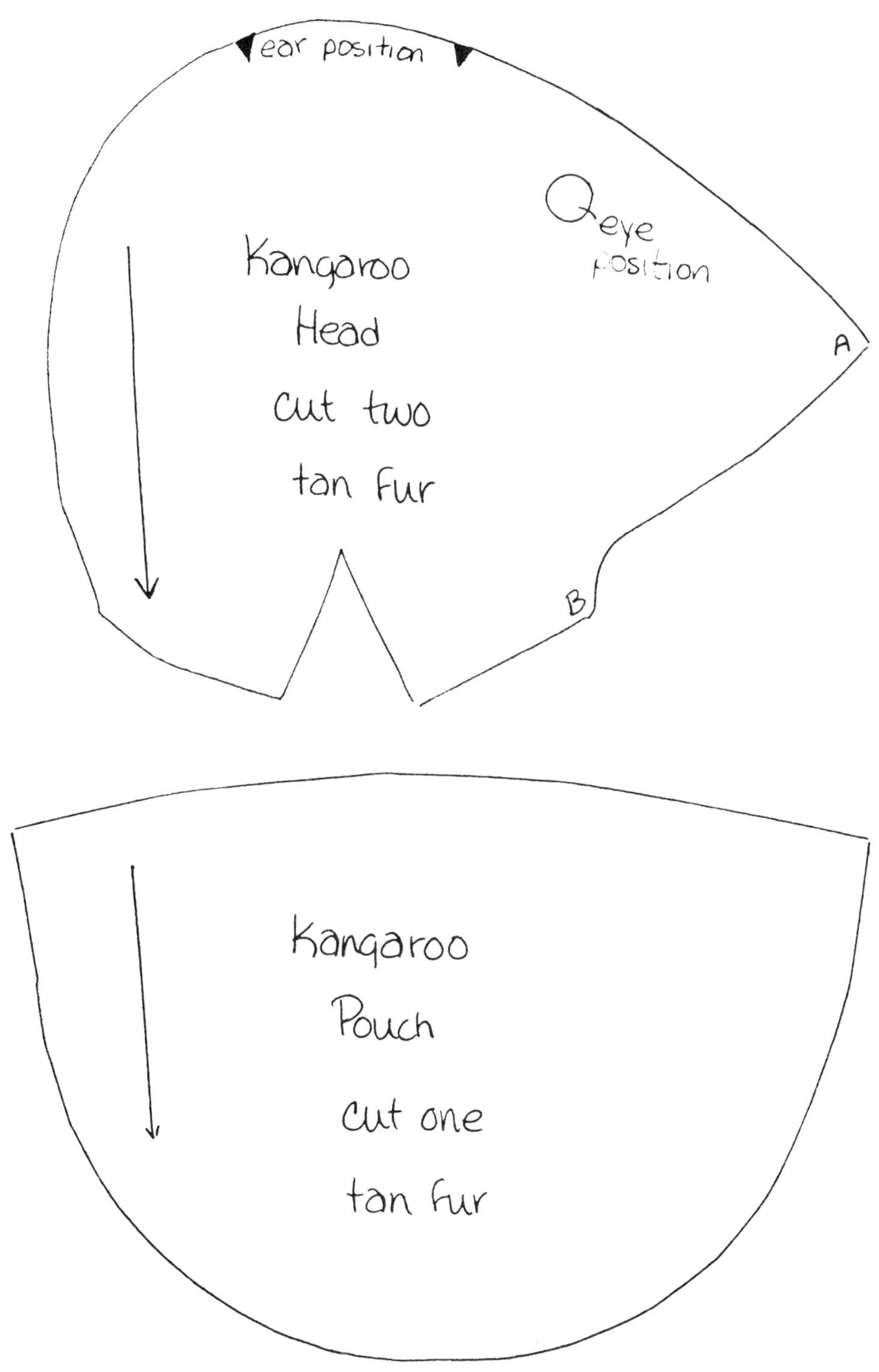

Illus. 66. Head and pouch patterns for Kristabel Kangaroo

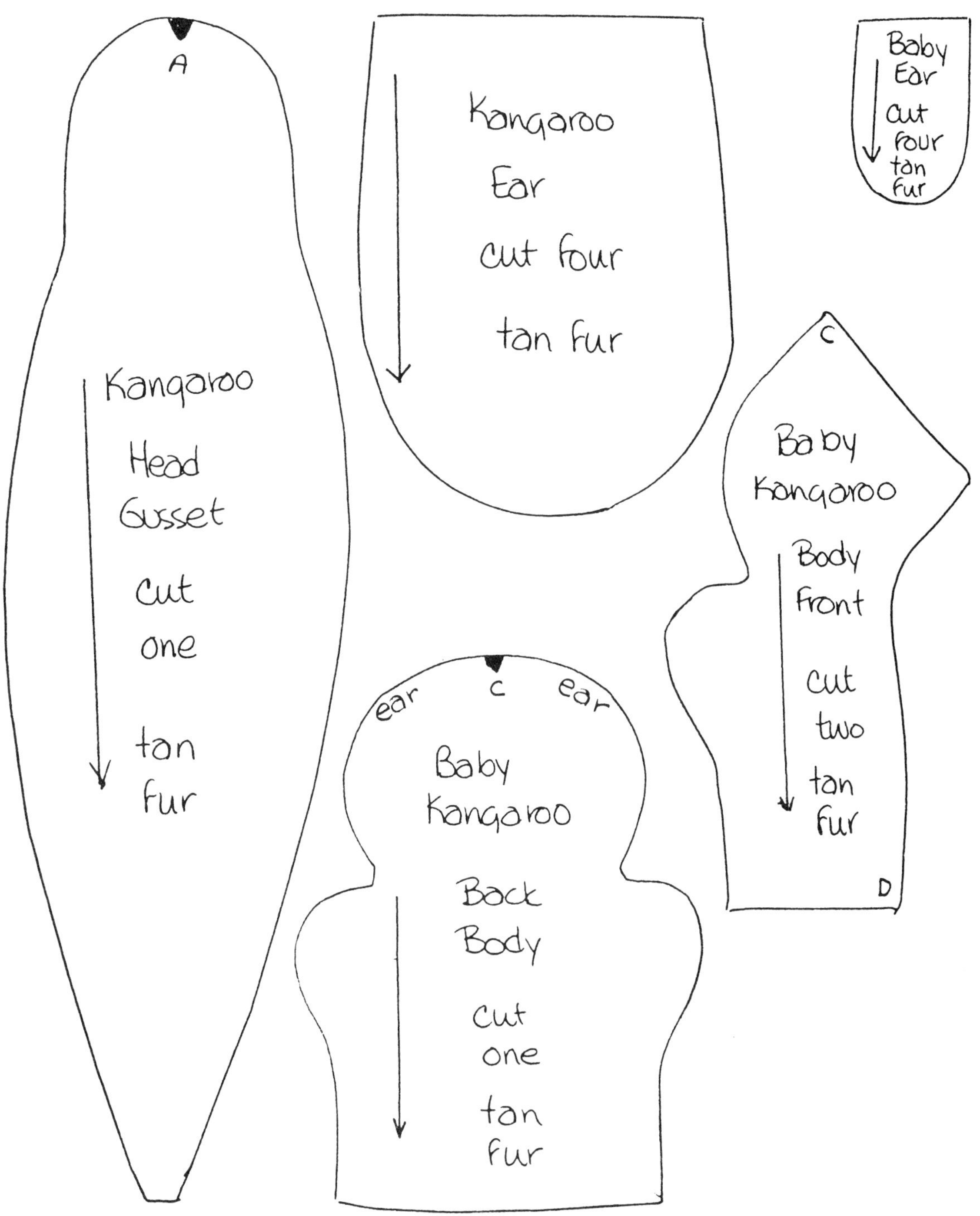

Illus. 67. Head gusset and ear patterns for Kristabel Kangaroo, and patterns for her baby

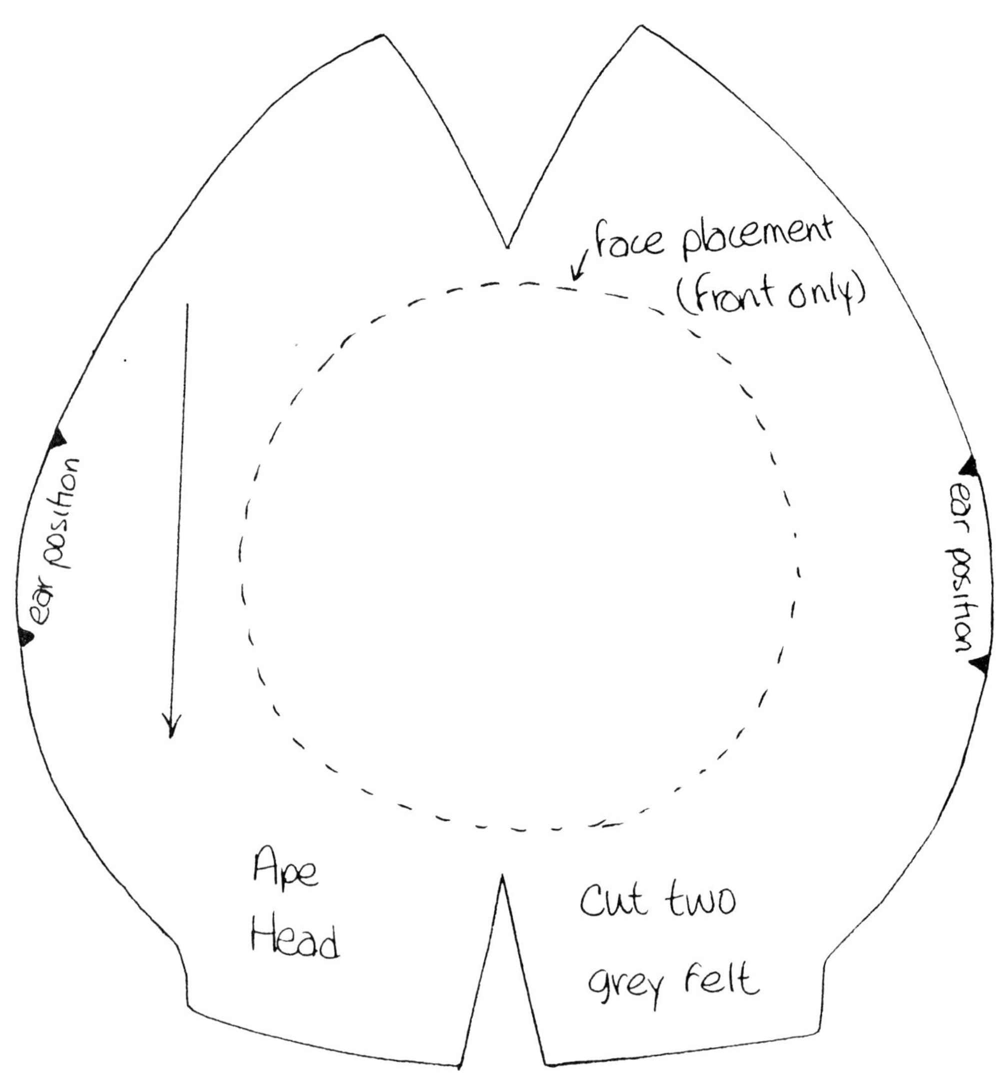

Illus. 68. Head pattern for Ashley Ape

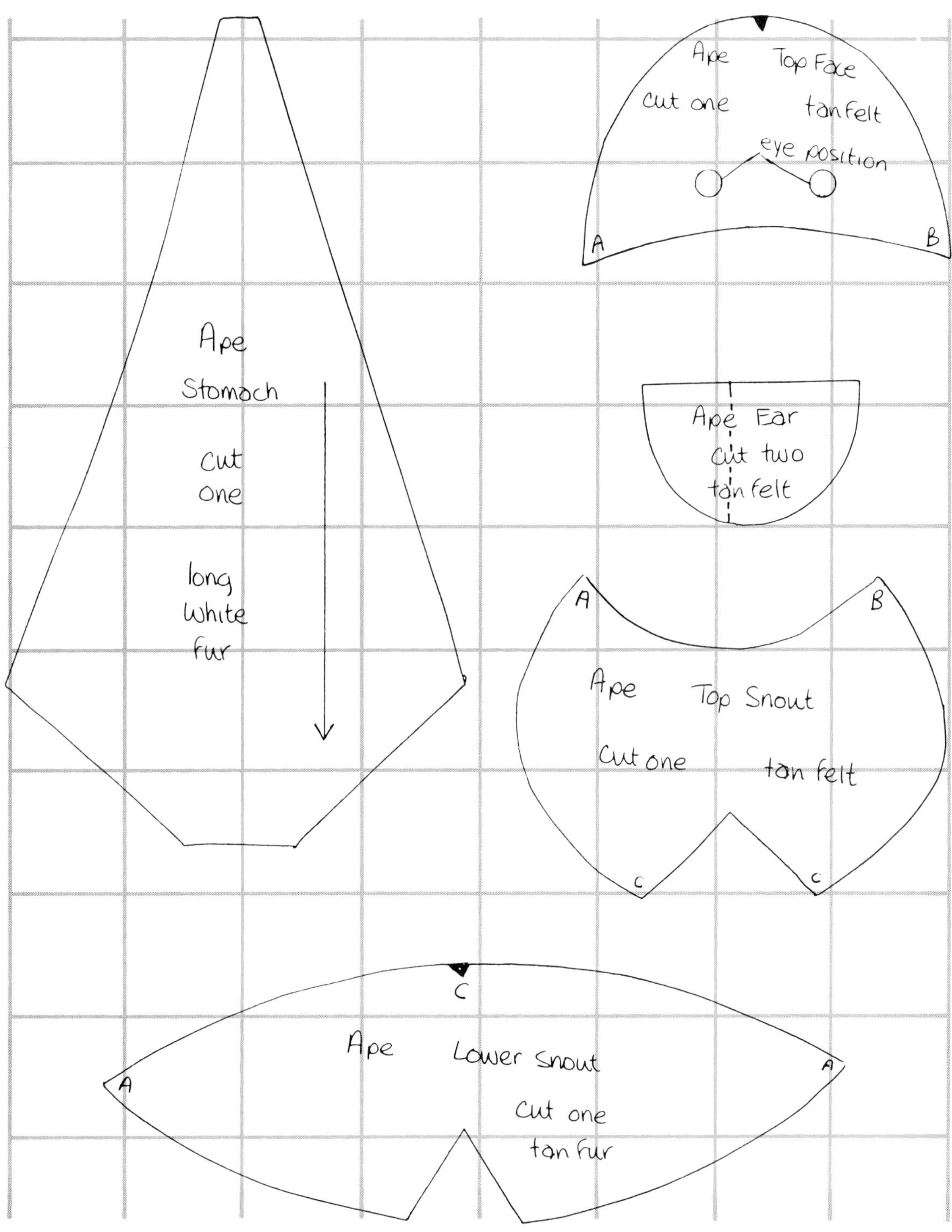

Illus. 69. Additional patterns for the Ape (75 percent of their original size)

· 5 ·
Mouth Puppets

Now familiar to almost everyone because of the Muppets, mouth puppets have the capacity to show facial manipulations, which makes them the most convincing speakers of the puppet world. Of all the different types of puppets, mouth puppets are probably the most enjoyable to use since they can "talk."

Although those presented here don't have the built-in option of limb manipulation, you can move their hands by using thin rods attached at their wrists, which you can manipulate with your free hand. This is a skill that takes some practice; however, most amateur puppeteers can learn to make convincing speaking motions with these puppets in a relatively short time.

Mouth Lining

A cardboard or plastic lining glued inside the puppet's mouth will stiffen the mouth so that it can be manipulated. You can obtain the materials from common sources; for example, you can get the cardboard from the front or back of a cereal box, and the plastic from a bottle of bleach. If you opt for cardboard, you may wish to glue the cardboard to a piece of felt or fabric interfacing to increase the life of the lining.

First complete the puppet according to the directions, and

then cut a cardboard or plastic lining, using the mouth pattern as a guide. Score the lining along a fold line with a pen or a dull knife. Fold along this line and then coat the entire inner surface of the mouth lining with a generous amount of glue. Before the glue dries, insert the mouth lining into the puppet, matching the glued surface to the inside surface of the mouth. Maneuvering the lining into position inside the puppet will take some practice. Use a glue that is somewhat slow to dry so that you will have time to move the mouth lining around, even after it's been in contact with the mouth.

Morgan the Dog

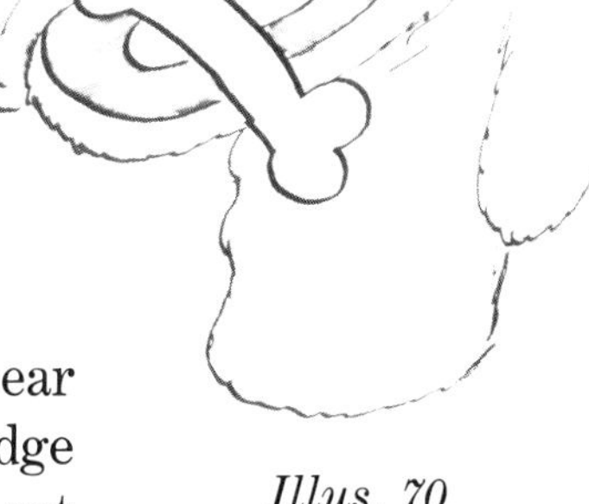

Illus. 70

Materials: 15″ × 25″ light-brown fur fabric
13″ × 9″ pink felt
2″ × 3″ dark-pink felt
scrap of brown felt
1 pair of brown plastic lock-in eyes, 15mm
cardboard or plastic
tiny amount of polyester stuffing

EARS: To make the ears, stitch the ear piece to the ear lining, with the right sides facing, leaving the straight edge at the top open. Turn the ears right side out and then set them aside.

TAIL: Stitch the tail pieces together, with the right sides facing, all around the curved edges, leaving the straight edge open. Turn and stuff lightly; then set aside.

BODY: Stitch darts in the top of the head and at the top of the nose, with the right sides facing. Baste the tail in position along the back seam of the body. Stitch the body pieces together, with the right sides facing, along the front seam (A-B), from the tip of the mouth, around the top of the head, and along the back (C-D), catching the tail in the stitching. Matching the notches on the mouth piece to points B-E-C-E on the mouth opening of the body-and-head pattern, stitch the mouth piece into the opening. Poke holes for the eye stems in the indicated positions on the body-and-head pattern; then apply the eyes by pushing the stems through from the right side and securing them with lock washers. Turn the dog right side out and then apply the mouth lining according to the instructions on page 76.

TO FINISH: Make the nose by using the circle technique on page 8 and then attach it to the front of the snout. Glue the tongue in position inside the mouth. Attach the ears by hand-stitching them along the lines indicated on the pattern.

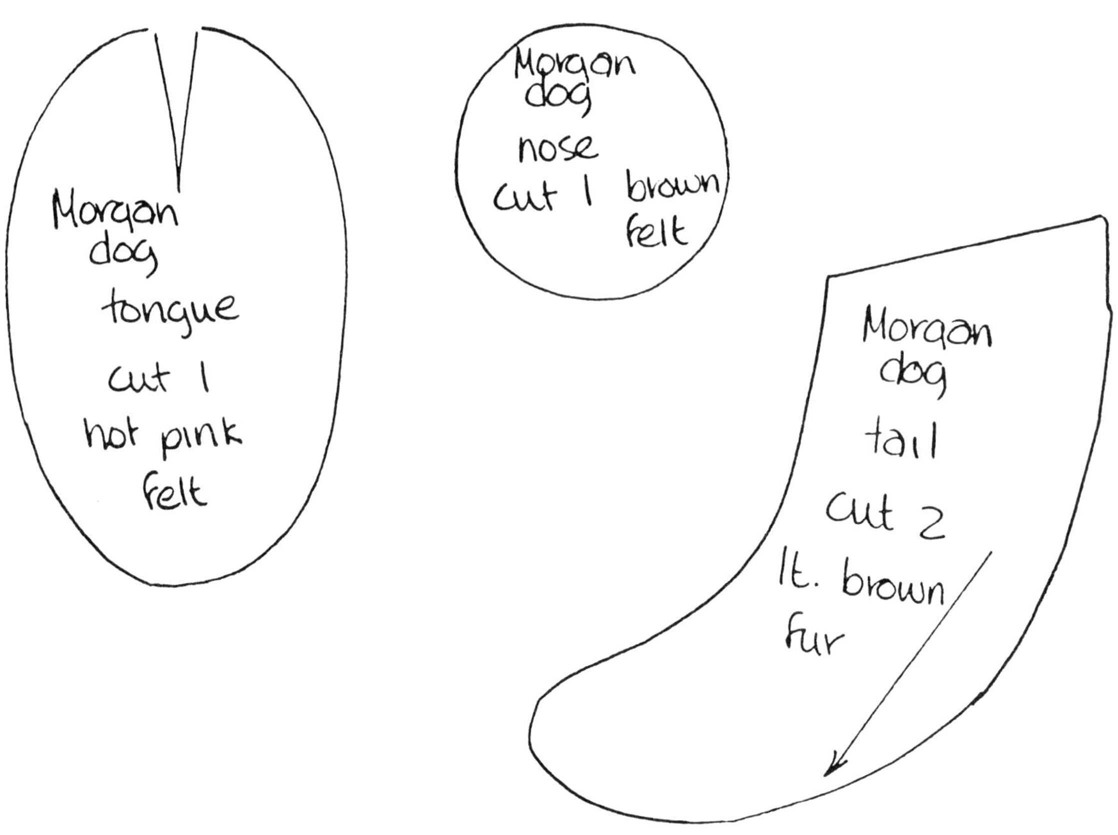

Illus. 71. Tongue, nose, and tail patterns for Morgan the Dog

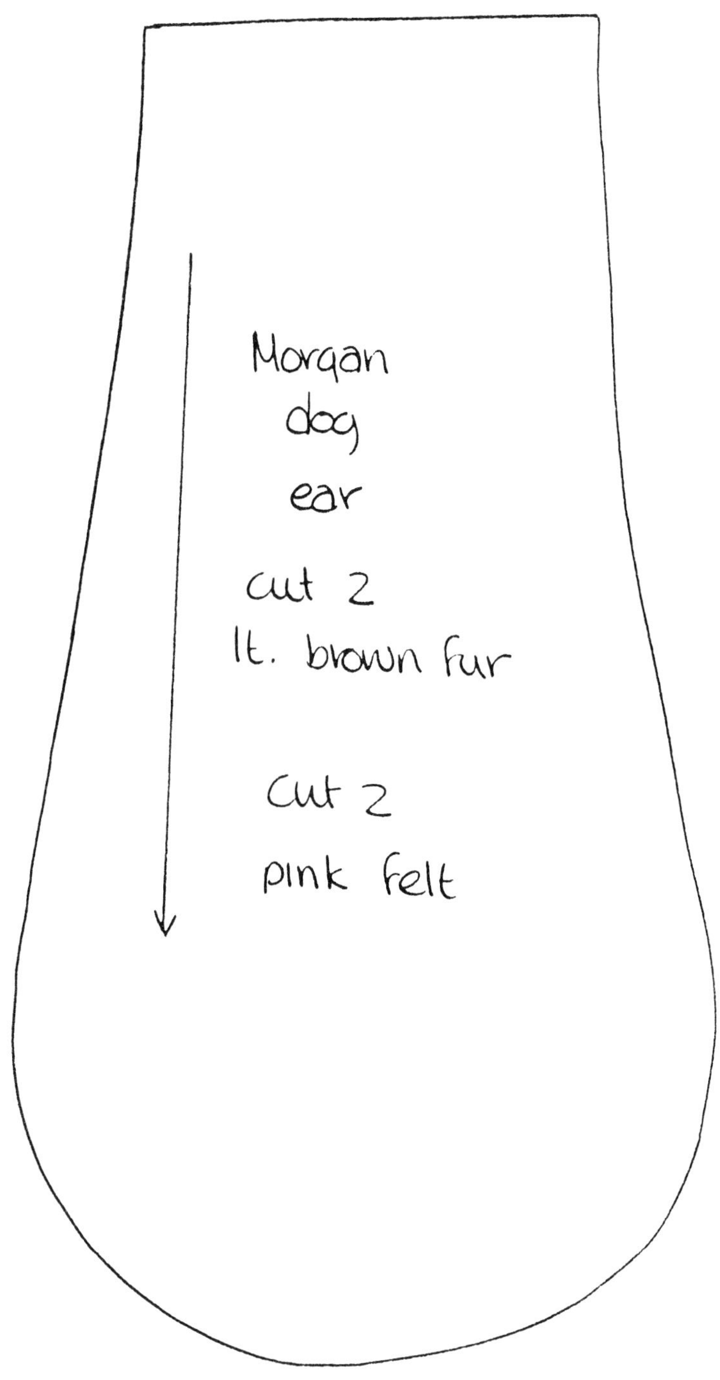

Illus. 72. Ear pattern for Morgan the Dog

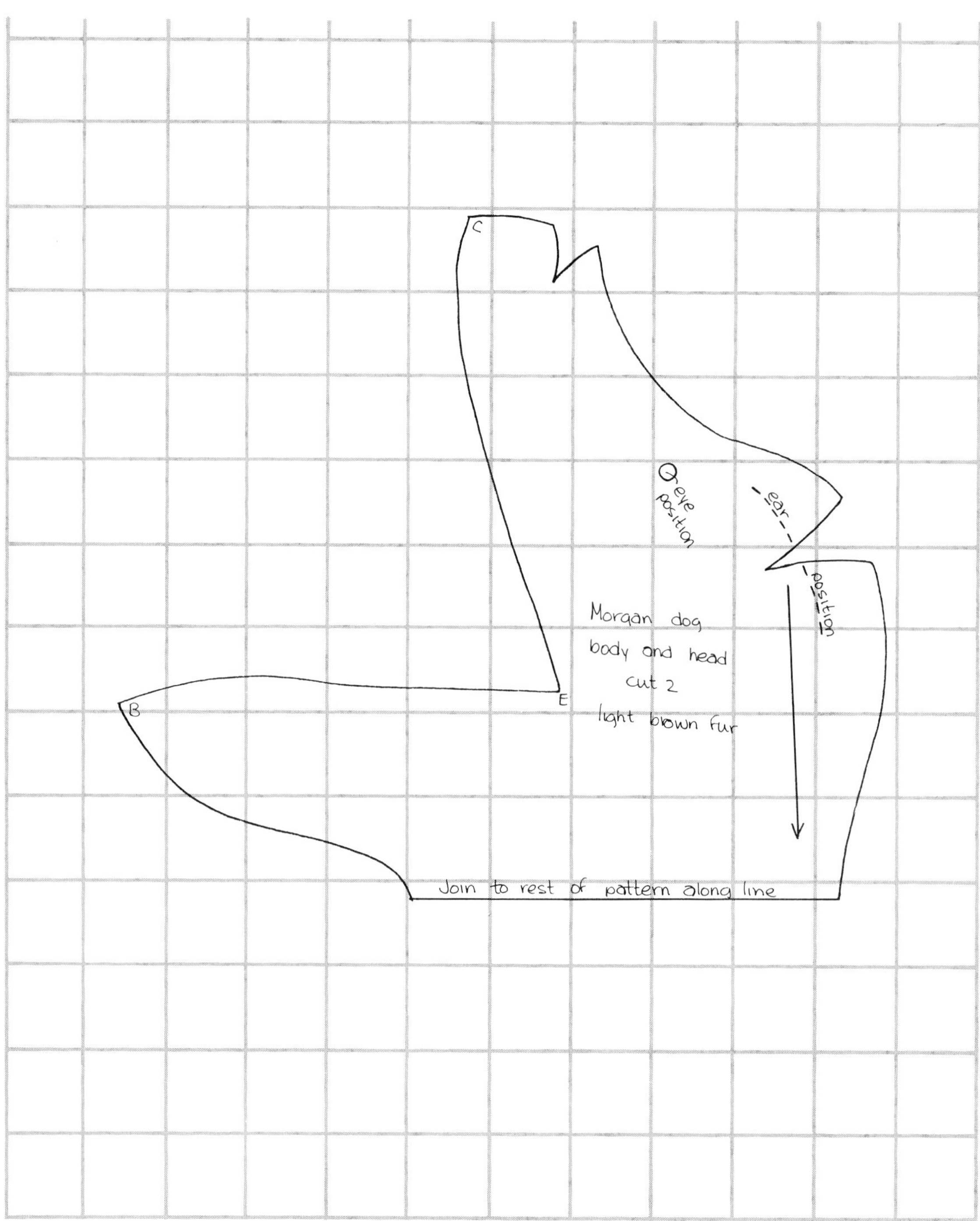

Illus. 73. Body-and-head pattern for Morgan the Dog (50 percent of its original size)

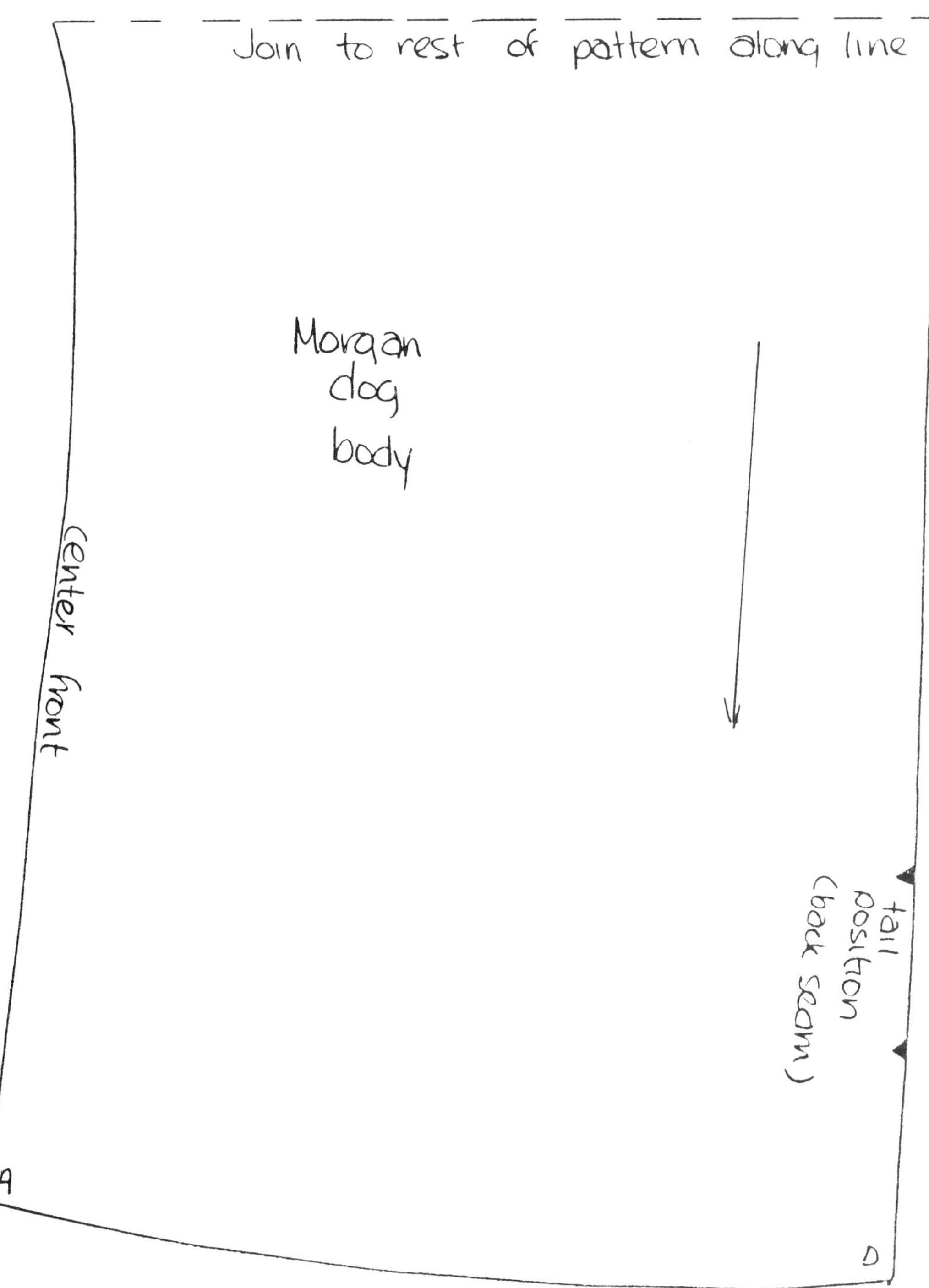

Illus. 74. Pattern for the rest of the body

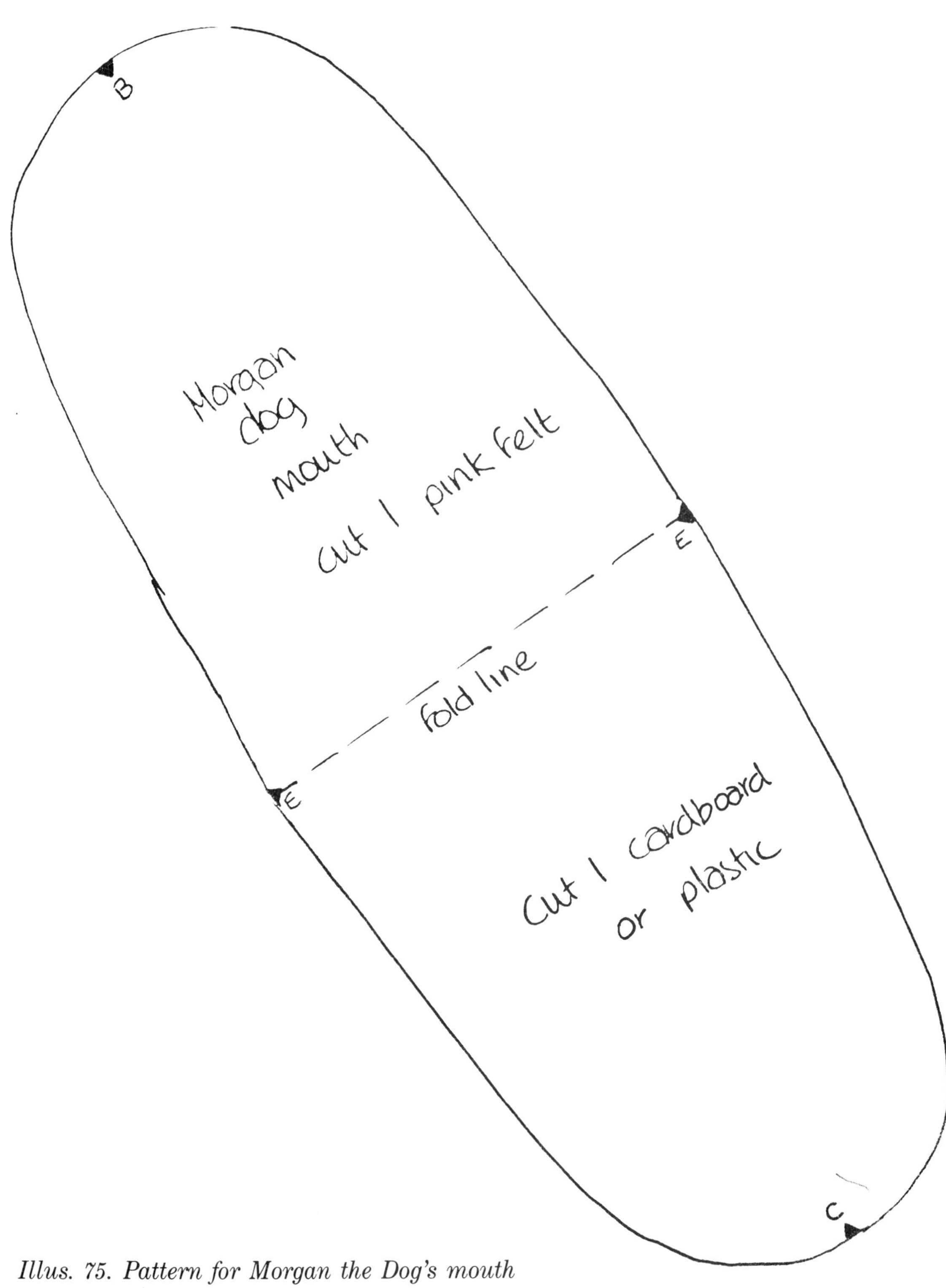

Illus. 75. Pattern for Morgan the Dog's mouth

Loretta Bird

Illus. 76

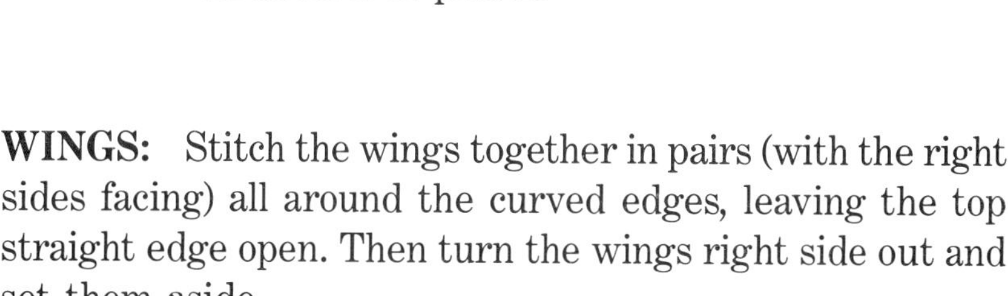

Materials: 12″ × 24″ yellow fur
8″ × 9″ orange felt
5″ × 10″ red felt
1 pair of fancy plastic lock-in eyes, 18mm
small amount of polyester fibre stuffing
cardboard or plastic

WINGS: Stitch the wings together in pairs (with the right sides facing) all around the curved edges, leaving the top straight edge open. Then turn the wings right side out and set them aside.

TAIL: Prepare the tail the same way you prepared the wings, but stuff it lightly. Set it aside.

BODY: Matching points A-B and C-B, stitch the upper and lower beak pieces to the body, with the right sides facing. Insert the wings, facing forward, into the slashes in the body, and then stitch the slashes closed, catching the tops of the wings in the stitching. Baste the tail in position along the body back. Stitch darts in the top of the body pieces. Next, stitch the body sides together along all edges, with the right sides facing and matching all points, catching the tail in the stitching and leaving the body open along mouth edges D-B-E and at the bottom. Matching points D-B-E-B on the body with the notches on the mouth piece, stitch the mouth into position. Poke holes for the eyes where they are indicated on the body; then insert the plastic eyes into position by pushing the stems through from the right side and fastening them with lock washers. Now turn the bird right side out. Turn up a narrow hem along the bottom of the puppet body. Stitch. Insert a cardboard or plastic mouth lining in position according to the instructions on page 76.

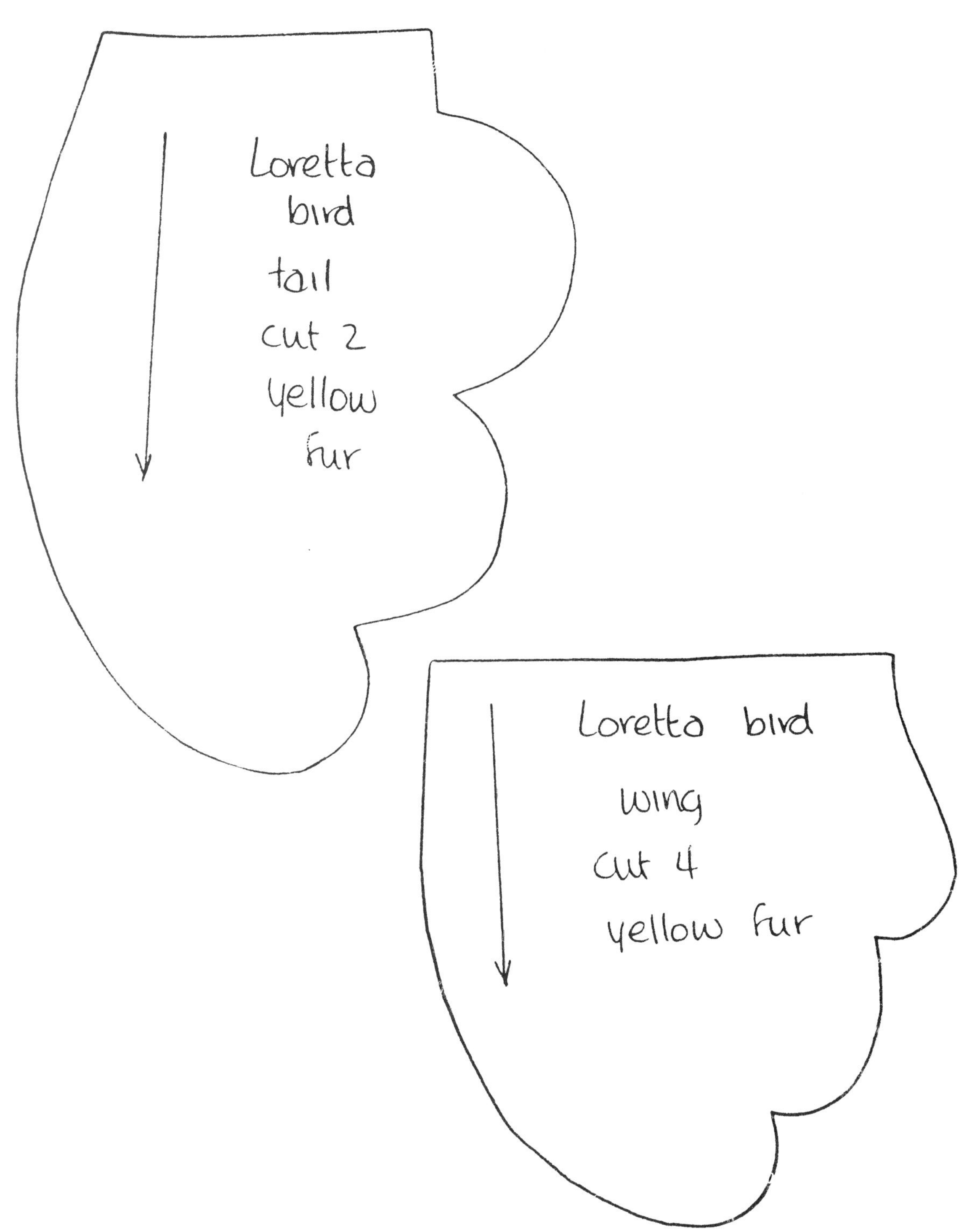

Illus. 77. Tail and wing patterns for Loretta Bird

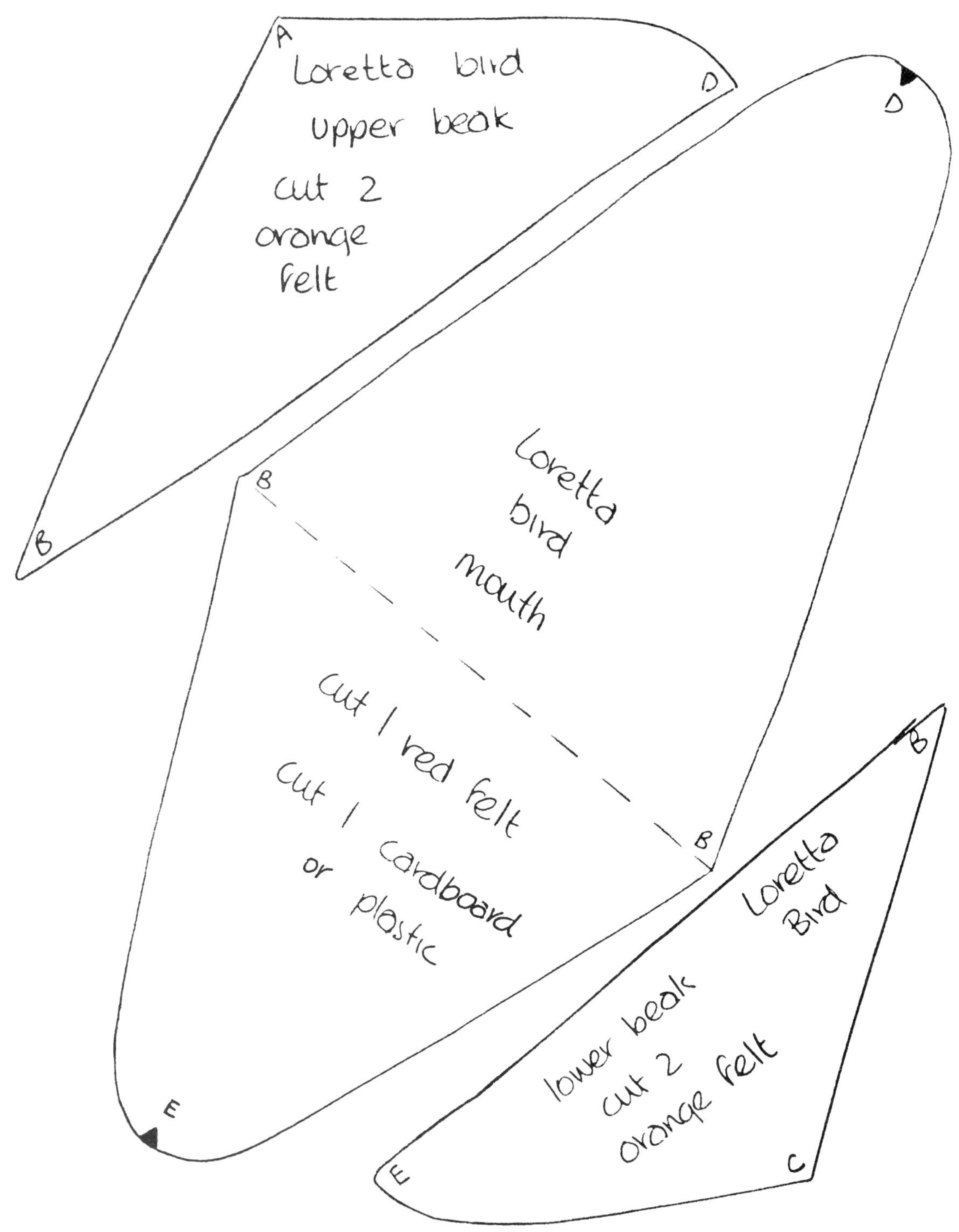

Illus. 78. Mouth and upper and lower beak patterns for Loretta Bird

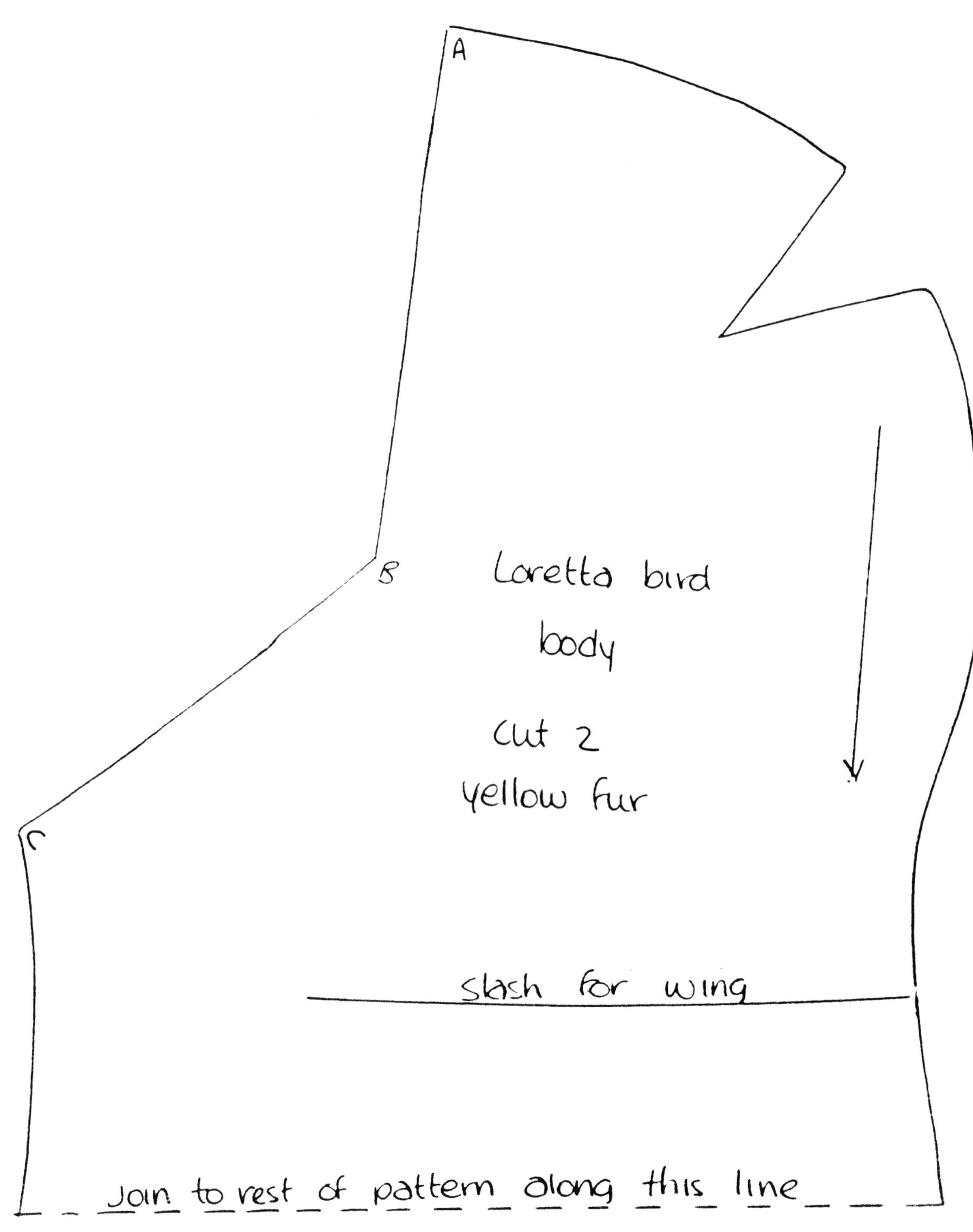

Illus. 79. Body pattern for Loretta Bird

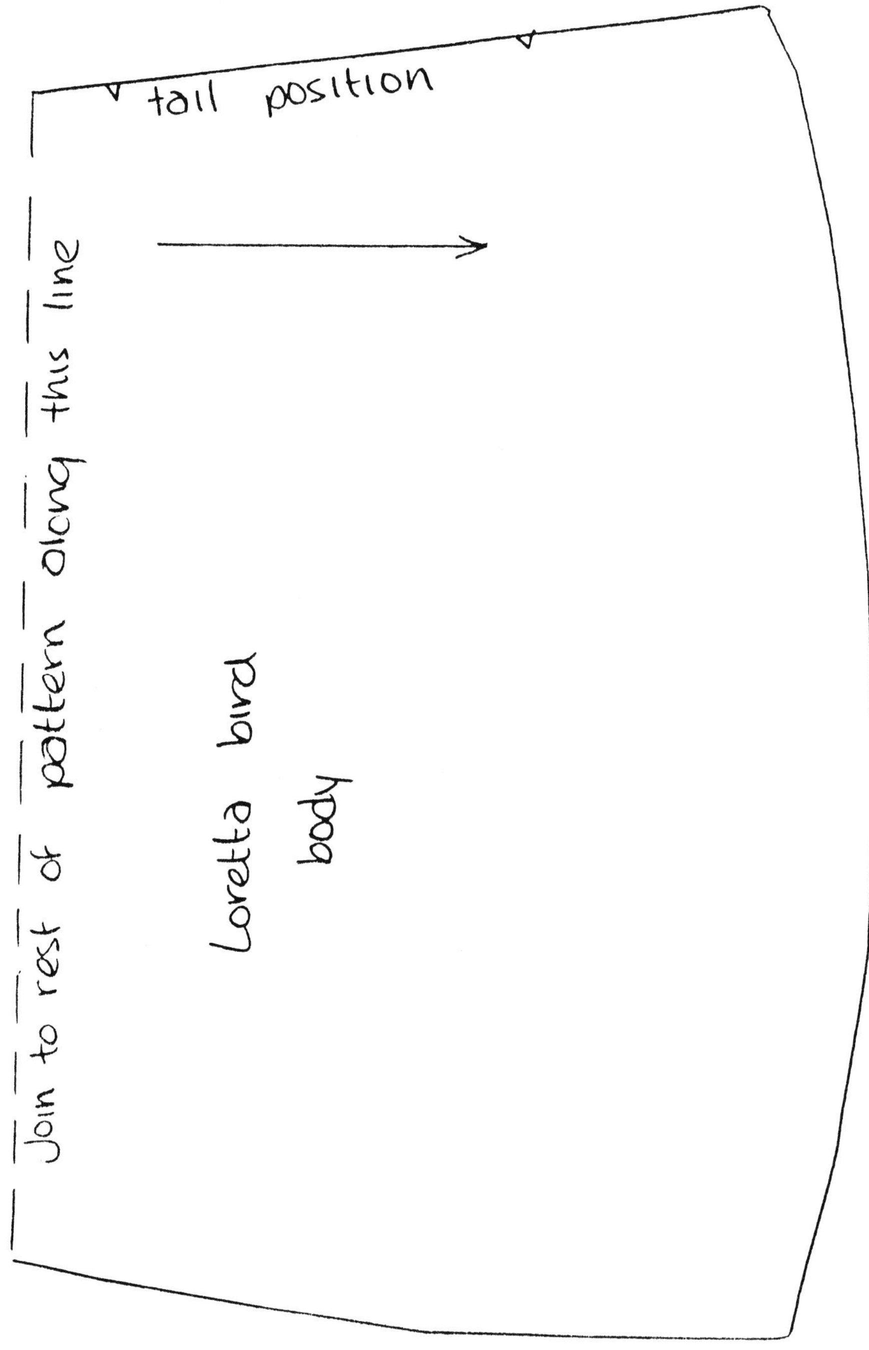

Illus. 80. Pattern for the rest of the body

Freddy Frog

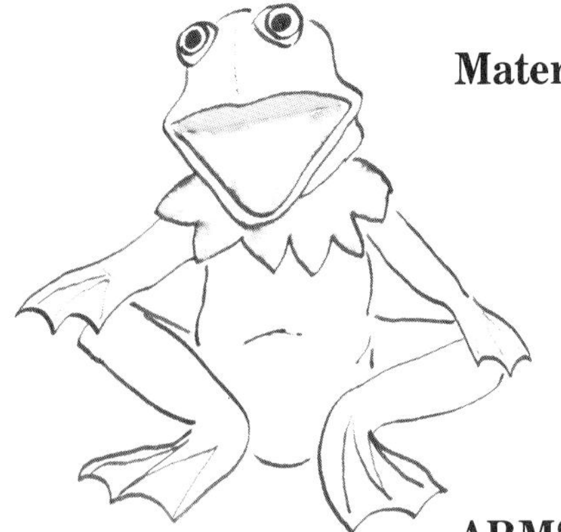

Illus. 81

Materials: 24″ × 30″ green felt
5″ × 5″ red felt
8″ × 8″ yellow felt
7″ × 11″ cotton fabric
1 pair of plastic lock-in frog eyes, 20mm
approximately ½ lb. polyester fibre stuffing
cardboard or plastic

ARMS: Stitch the arms together in pairs (with the *wrong* sides facing), down one edge, across at the wrist, and up the other edge. Stitch the webbed lines along the "hands," as indicated on the pattern piece. Lightly stuff the arms to within 1 inch of the top and then set them aside.

LEGS: Stitch the legs the same way you stitched the arms. Fill the legs to the knees, and stitch across to form the hinge. Fill the legs to within 1 inch of the top and then set them aside.

COLLAR: Topstitch all around the edge of the collar and then set it aside.

BODY: Stitch darts in the head. Insert the arms, angled downwards, into the slashes on the sides of the body. Stitch the slashes closed, catching the arms in the line of stitching. Insert the legs, angled upwards, into the darts on the lower body. Stitch the darts closed, catching the legs in the line of stitching. Stitch the body sides together, with the right sides facing, leaving the body open at the bottom and along mouth-edge A-B-C. Stitch the mouth into position, with the right sides facing and matching points A-B-C-B. Poke holes for the eyes where they are marked on the pattern; then insert the eyes from the right side by pushing the stems through the holes and fastening them with lock washers. If you can't find plastic eyes for a frog, you can make the eyes from felt using the circle technique on page 8 and then attach them after the frog is completed.

Prepare the body lining by folding the body pattern in half widthwise so that the shorter edges meet. Stitch this seam. Insert the lining into the bottom of the puppet body, matching the raw edges; then stitch the lining and the body together, leaving about 1 inch open. Turn the puppet right side out.

Tuck the lining against the inside of the puppet. Slip the collar over the head and into position. Hand-stitch the collar in position on the neck of the puppet, catching the lining to the inside of the puppet. Keep your hand inside the puppet while you are stitching to be sure that you don't stitch the neck closed. Now apply the mouth lining, following the instructions on page 76.

Lightly stuff the lower body through the 1-inch opening to create a sort of "tummy" effect. Hand-stitch the opening closed, and fold the legs to the front. Then catch the heels to the front of the tummy with a few stitches.

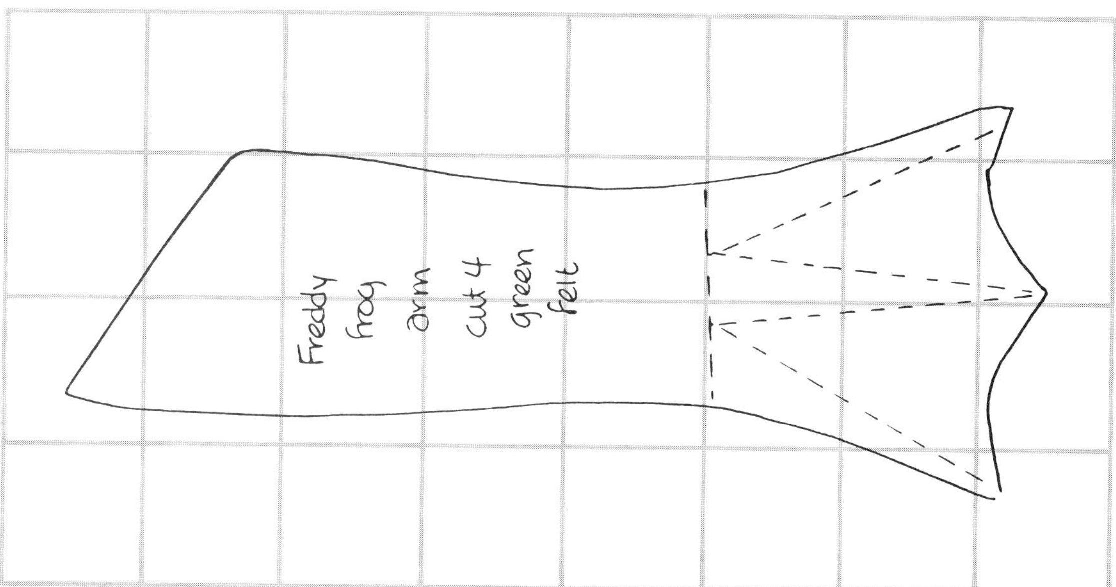

Illus. 82. Arm pattern for Freddy the Frog (75 percent of its original size)

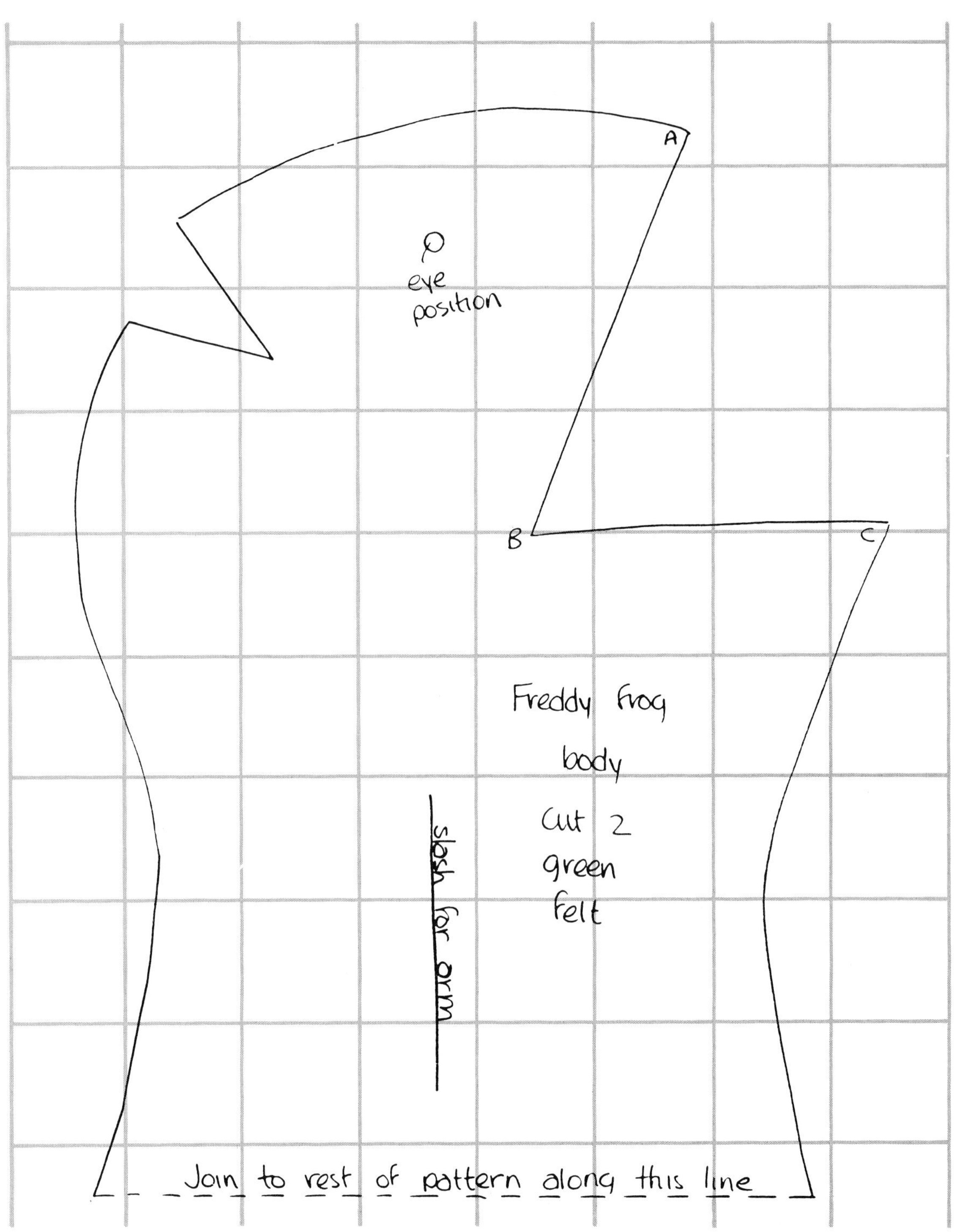

Illus. 83. Body pattern for Freddy the Frog (75 percent of its original size)

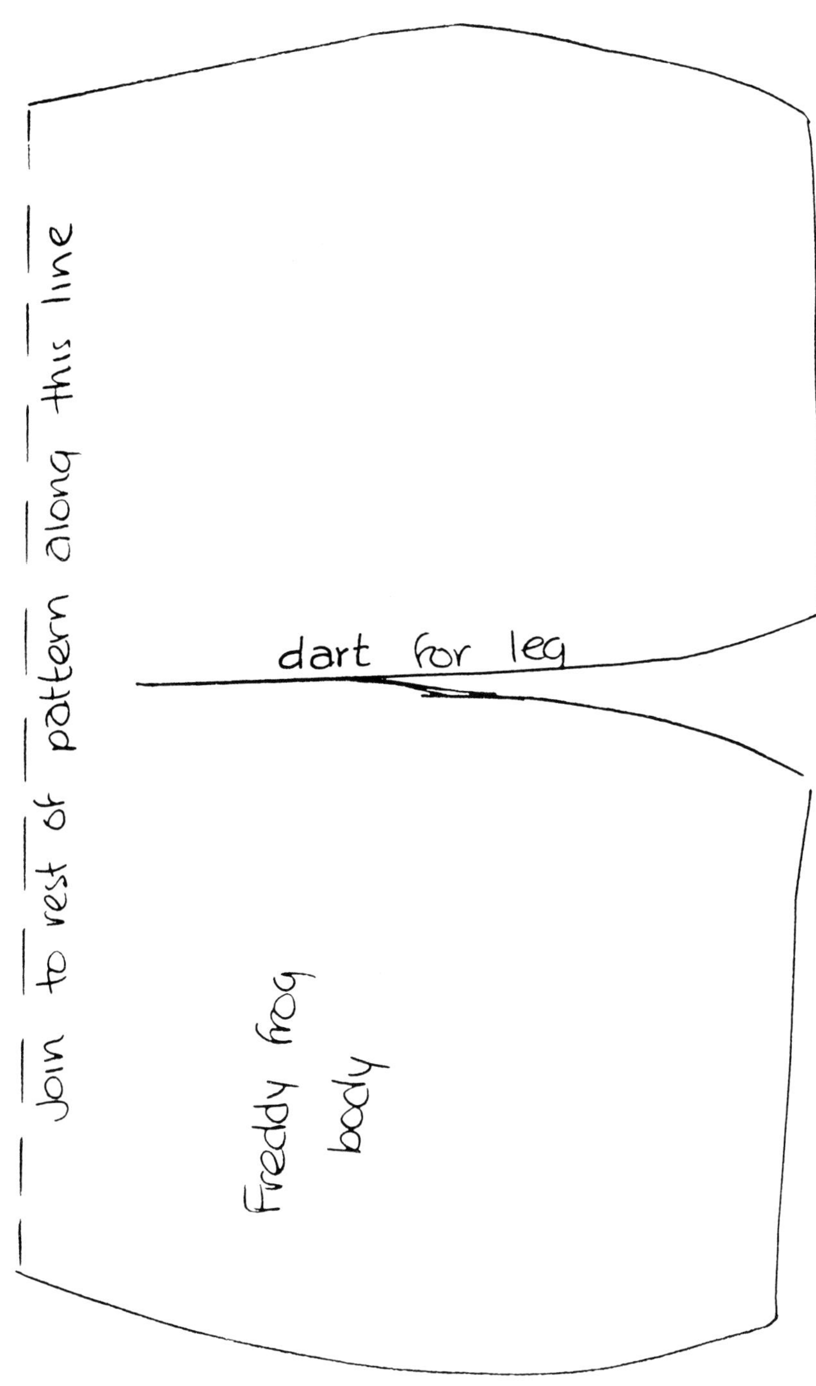

Illus. 84. Pattern for the rest of the body

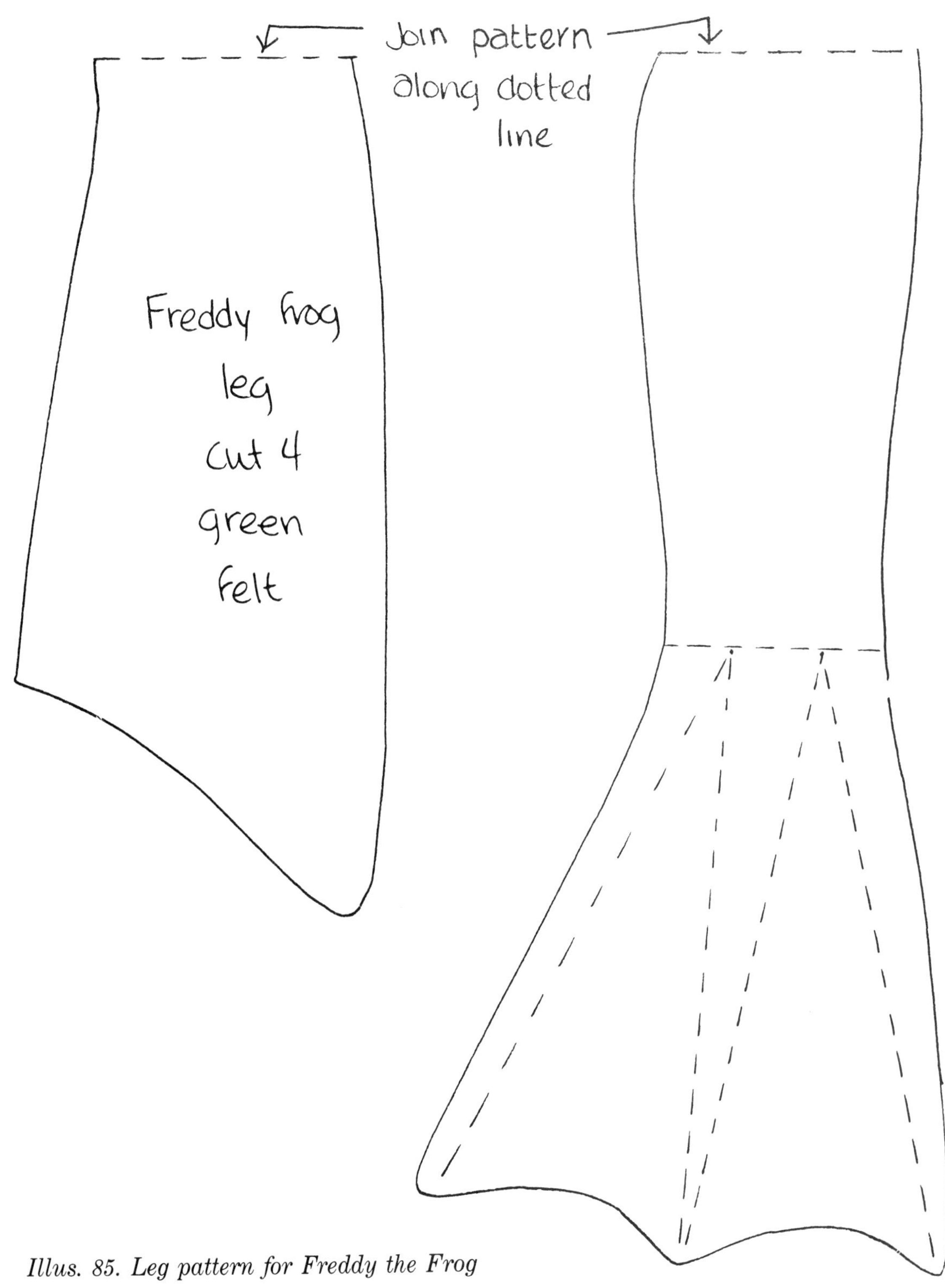

Illus. 85. Leg pattern for Freddy the Frog

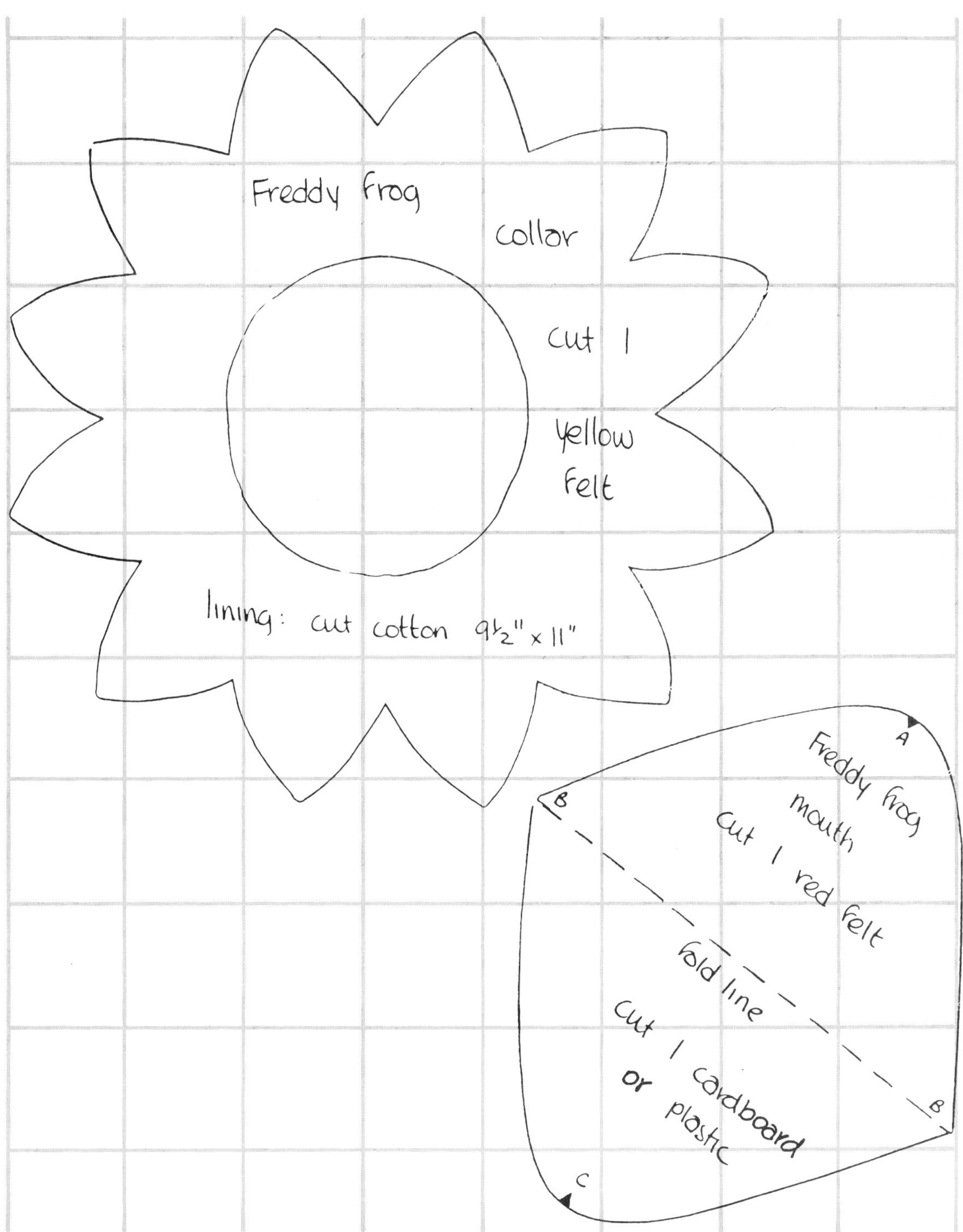

Illus. 86. Patterns for Freddy the Frog's collar and mouth (75 percent of their original size)

Illus. 87

Harry Monster

Materials: 18″ × 24″ lime-green long-pile fur fabric
15″ × 20″ hot-pink long-pile fur fabric
2 ping-pong balls (for eyeballs)
2″ × 5″ red felt
1 pair of plastic vampire teeth
small amount of polyester fibre stuffing
cardboard or plastic

Note: It is difficult to work with long-pile fur fabric, so use extra care in handling it. You may want to keep a hairbrush nearby, and, at intervals, brush the long pile out of the way of the seams.

ARMS: To make the arms, stitch together one arm piece of each color, with the right sides facing, leaving the top open. Then turn the arms right side out and lightly stuff.

BODY: Baste the arms in position (with the green sides uppermost), along the lower half of the side body. Stitch the upper half of the side body to the lower half of the side body along A-B, with the right sides facing and matching edges, catching the arms in the stitching. Stitch the head darts. Next, stitch the stomach piece to the side body along C-D, with the right sides facing and matching edges.

Stitch the monster body together, with the right sides facing, along front seam line E-F, then along top-and-back G-H, leaving the body open along the mouth. Matching points E-C-G-C, stitch the mouth into position. Then turn the monster right side out.

Separate the upper and lower teeth by cutting them apart along the fold. Glue the teeth in position along the front edges of the mouth. For extra security, use strong thread to stitch the teeth in position.

Make the mouth lining from cardboard strengthened with interfacing, following the instructions on page 76. Since this puppet's head is so large, you will need to attach pockets to the mouth lining so that the mouth can be manipulated effectively. These pockets are for the puppeteer's fingers and thumb. Cut the pocket pieces from interfacing, and stitch them in position all around the mouth lining piece, matching points J-K. Now insert the mouth piece into position, according to the directions on page 77.

EYES: Glue the eyebrows to the eyeballs. Spread glue over the backs of the eyeballs, and stick them in position on the monster's face. You may want to stitch the eyebrows to the face for extra security. Glue the pupils in position on the eyeballs. Now you can groom the monster by brushing.

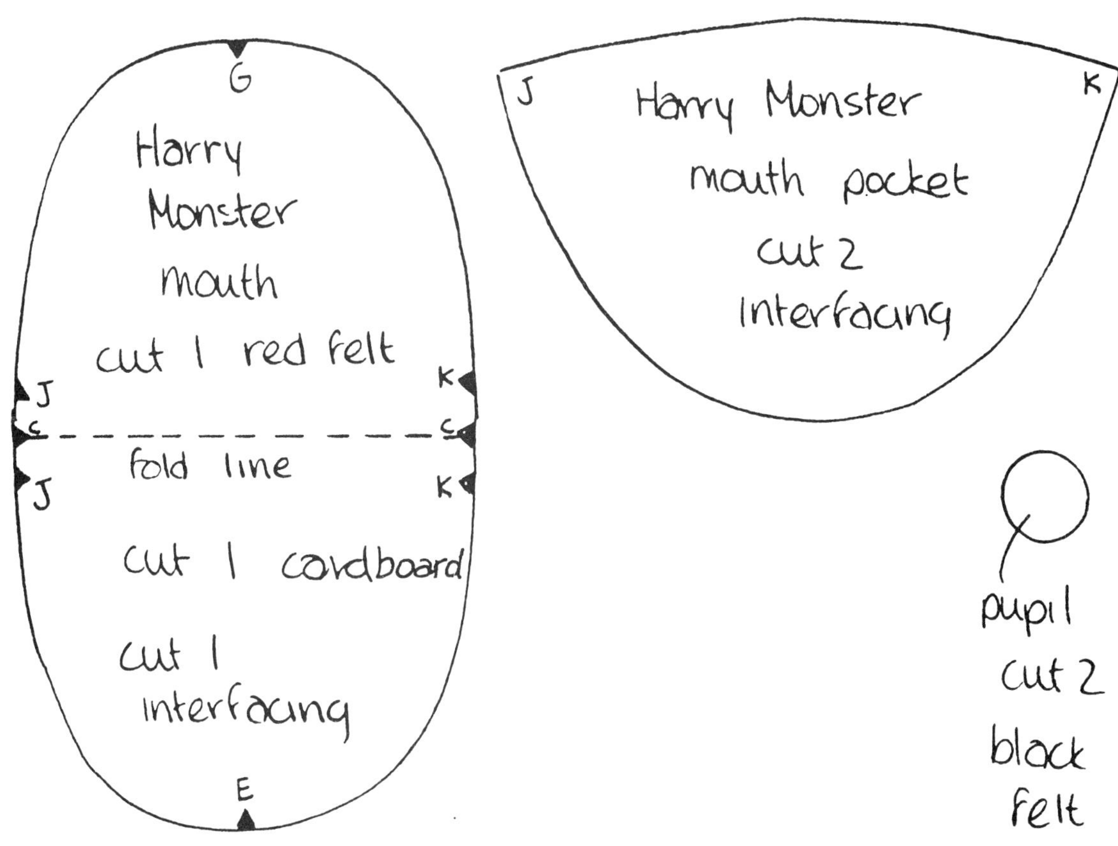

Illus. 88. Mouth, mouth pocket, and pupil patterns for Harry Monster

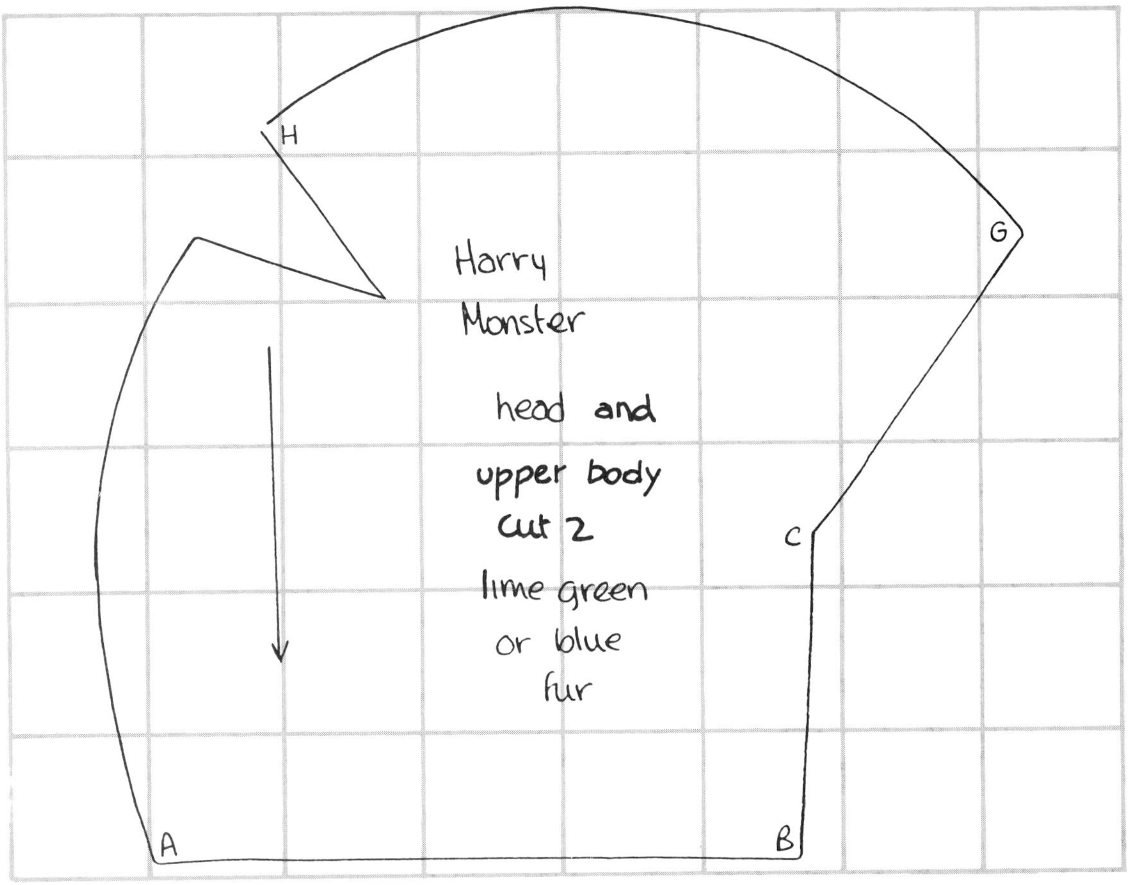

H

G

Harry
Monster

head and
upper body
cut 2
lime green
or blue
fur

C

A

B

Illus. 89. Pattern for Harry Monster's head and upper body (75 percent of its original size)

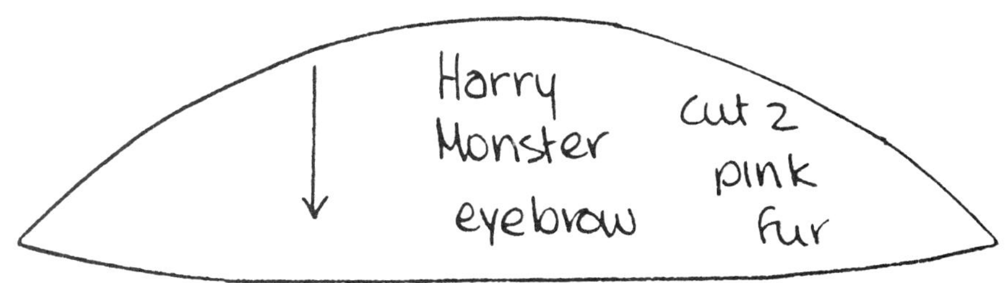

Illus. 90. Eyebrow pattern for Harry Monster

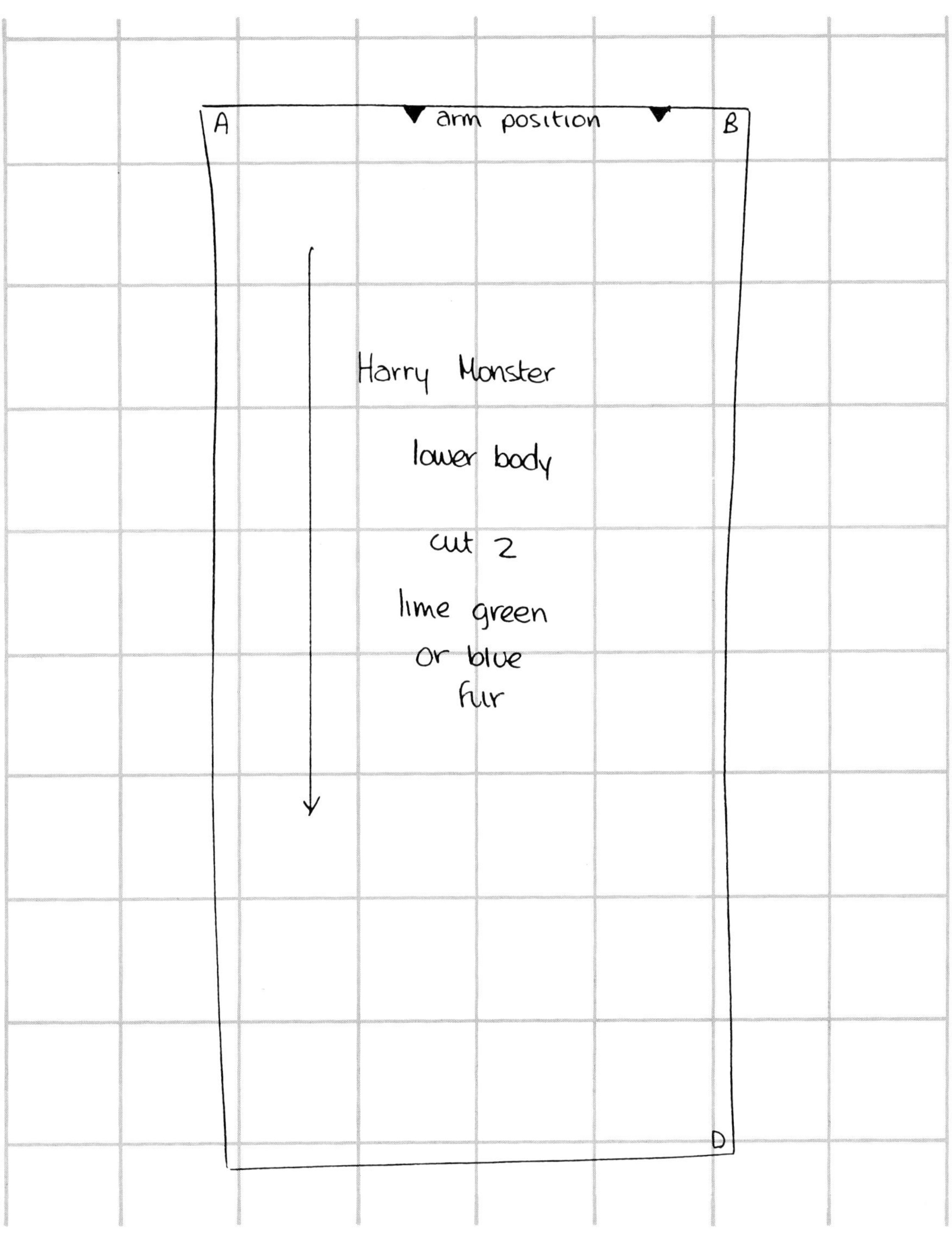

Illus. 91. Pattern for Harry Monster's lower body (75 percent of its original size)

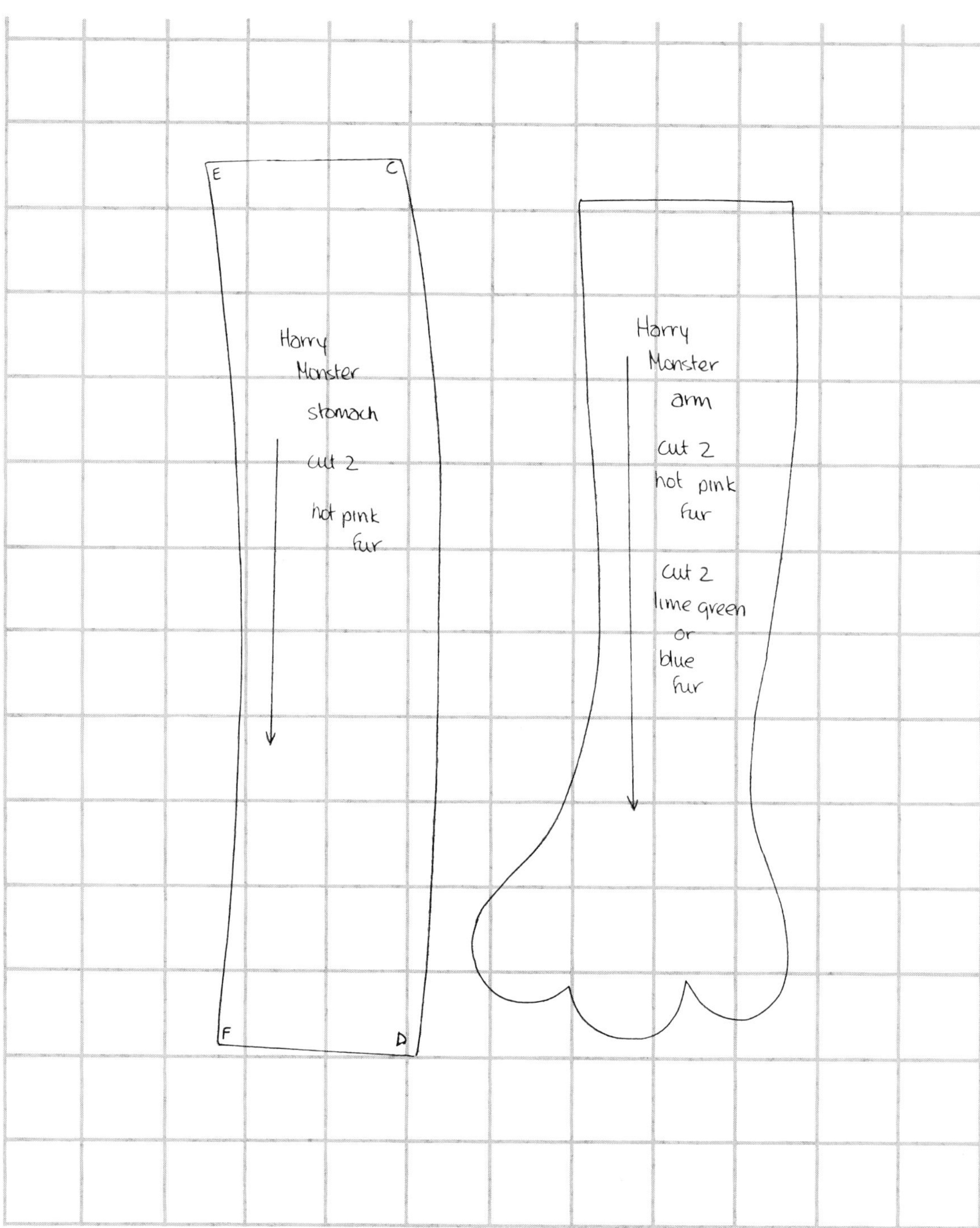

Illus. 92. Stomach and arm patterns for Harry Monster (50 percent of their original size)

Dennis the Indomitable Dragon

Illus. 93.

Materials: 15″ × 25″ dark-pink felt
13″ × 15″ light-pink felt
2″ × 8″ white felt
scrap of brown felt
chenille stem, 12″ long, any color
1 pair of plastic lock-in eyes, 15mm
cardboard or plastic
tiny amount of polyester stuffing

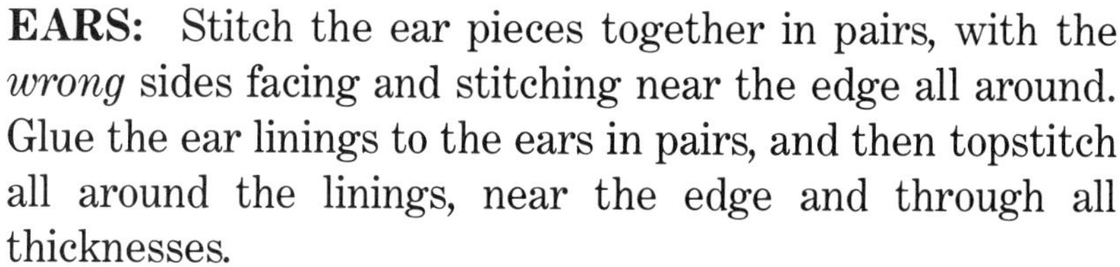

EARS: Stitch the ear pieces together in pairs, with the *wrong* sides facing and stitching near the edge all around. Glue the ear linings to the ears in pairs, and then topstitch all around the linings, near the edge and through all thicknesses.

TONGUE: With the wrong sides facing, stitch the tongue pieces together around the edges, leaving the straight edge open. Insert a chenille stem into the tongue, pushing all the way up.

BODY: Fold the stomach piece, with the wrong sides facing, along the lines indicated on the pattern. Topstitch near the fold lines to form small tucks. Stitch the stomach to the body front along A-B, with the right sides facing. Baste the ears into position, with the right sides facing; then stitch darts in the top of the head and at the nose top, catching the ears in the stitching. Baste the scales in position along the back seam of the body. Stitch the body pieces together, with the right sides facing, from the tip of the mouth, around the top of the head, and along the back (C-D), catching the scales in your stitching. Now stitch under chin-seam E-F. Fold the chin out of the way and stitch across the top of the stomach piece, with the right sides facing, under the chin (A-F-A).

MOUTH: Make a small slit where indicated on the mouth

piece and insert the tongue from the right side. Stitch the slit closed, catching the tongue in your stitching (you may want to do this by hand). Baste the teeth into position along the edges of the mouth. Matching notches on the mouth piece to points C-G-E-G on the mouth opening, stitch the mouth piece into the opening on the body, catching the teeth in your stitching. Next, glue the eyelids to the top of the eyes. Poke holes for the eye stems in the position indicated on the dragon body, and apply the eyes by pushing the stems through from the right side and securing them with lock washers. Now turn the dragon right side out and apply the mouth lining according to the instructions on page 76.

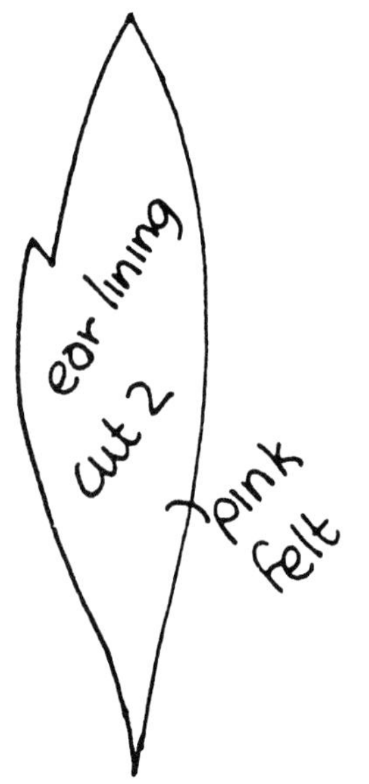

TO FINISH: Make the horn by stitching the two pieces together, with the right sides facing, leaving the bottom open. Then attach the horn to the front of the snout. Make the nostrils by hand-stitching a small circular tuck along the lines indicated on the pattern.

Illus. 94. Ear, ear lining, eyelid, and horn patterns for Dennis the Indomitable Dragon

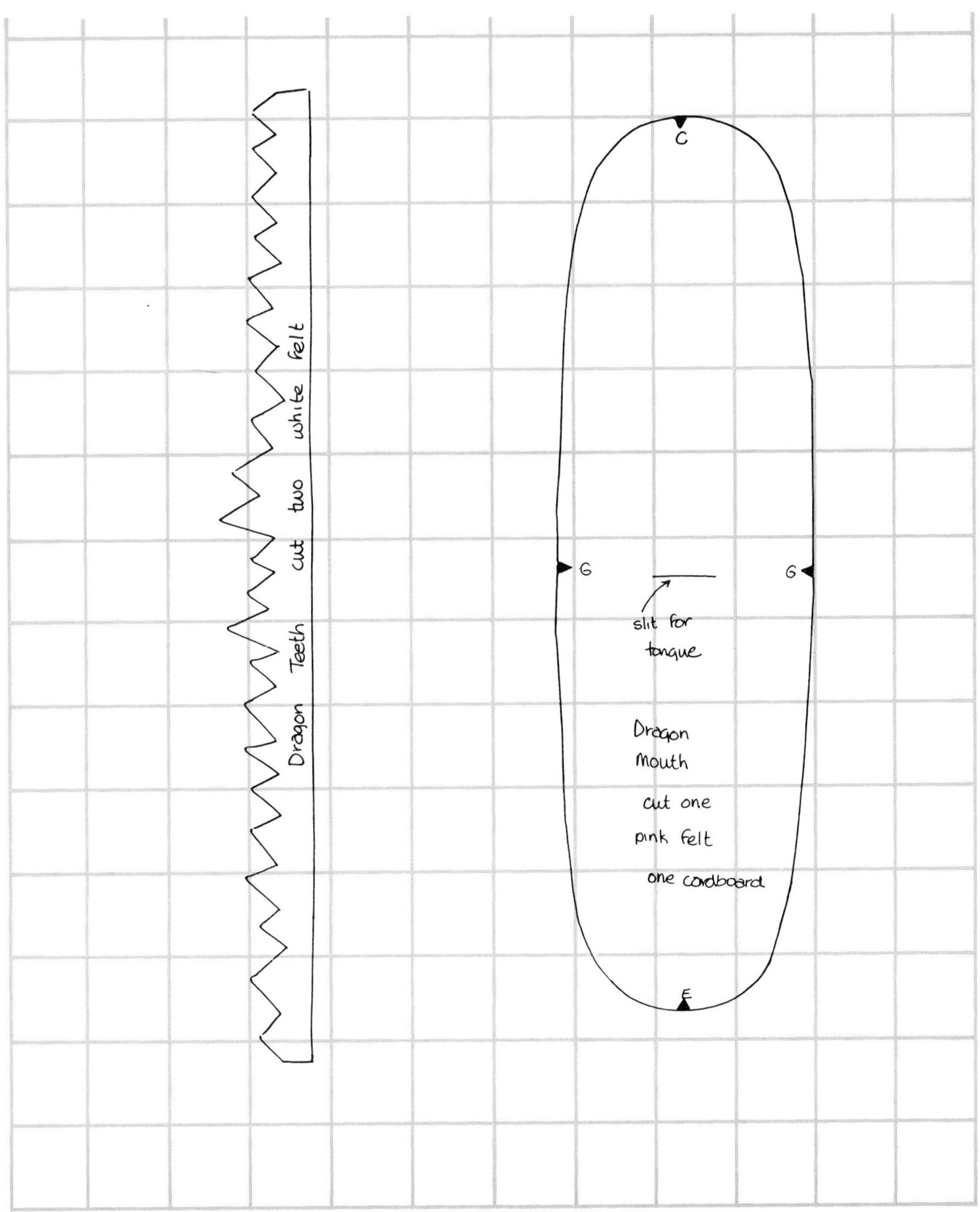

Illus. 95. Teeth and mouth patterns for the Dragon (50 percent of their original size)

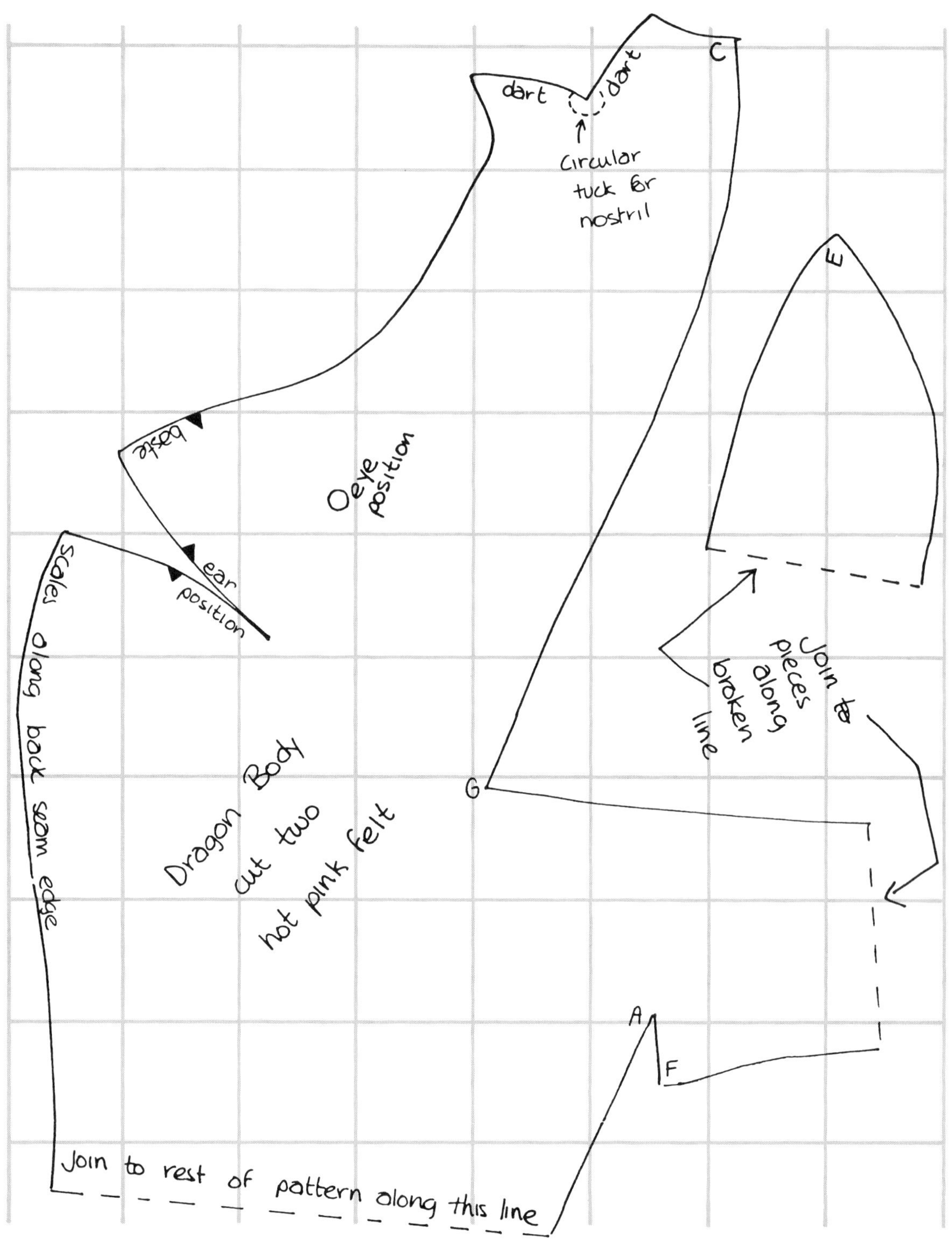

Illus. 96. Body pattern for the Dragon (75 percent of its original size)

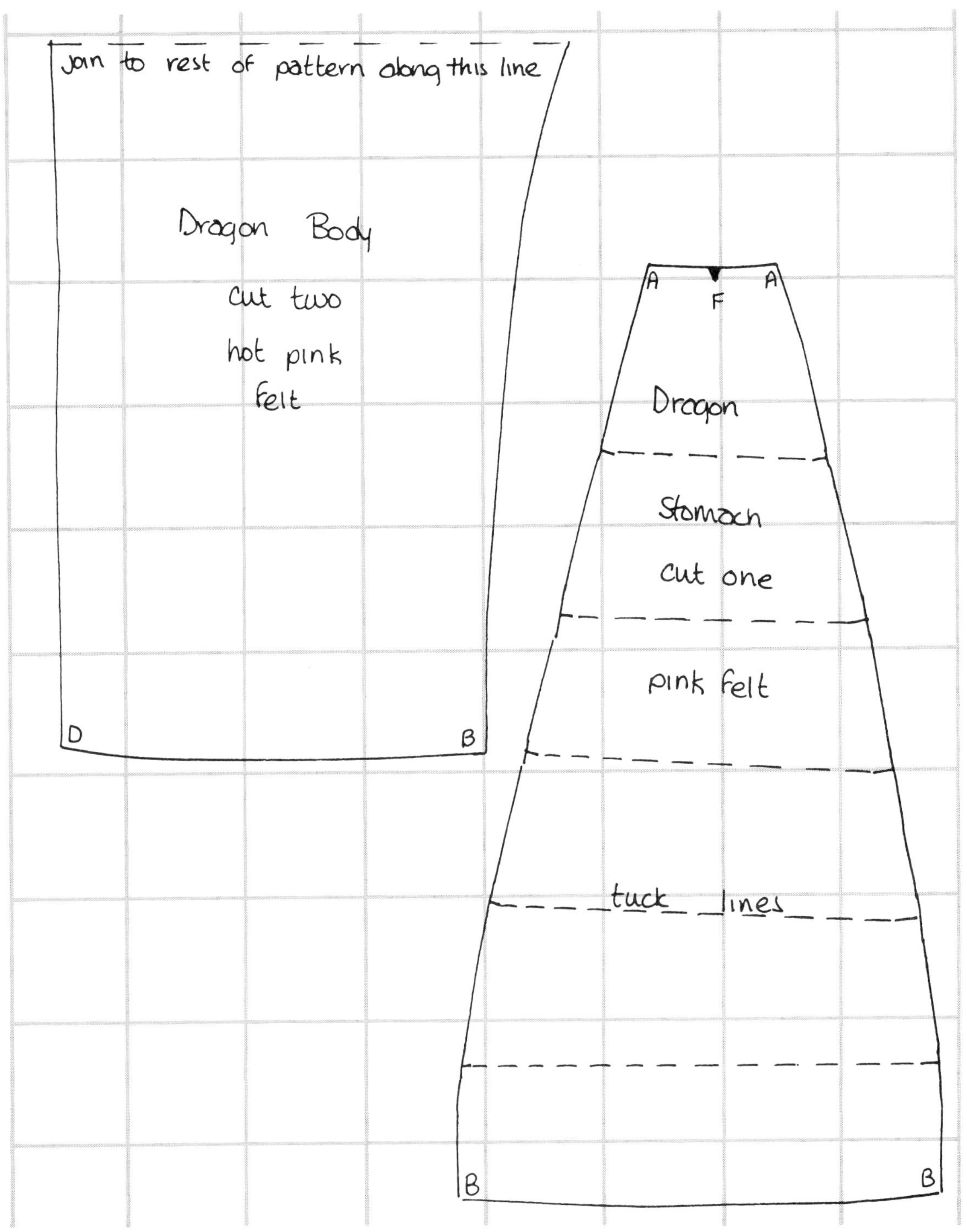

Illus. 97. Pattern for the rest of the Dragon's body, and pattern for the Dragon's stomach (75 percent of their original size)

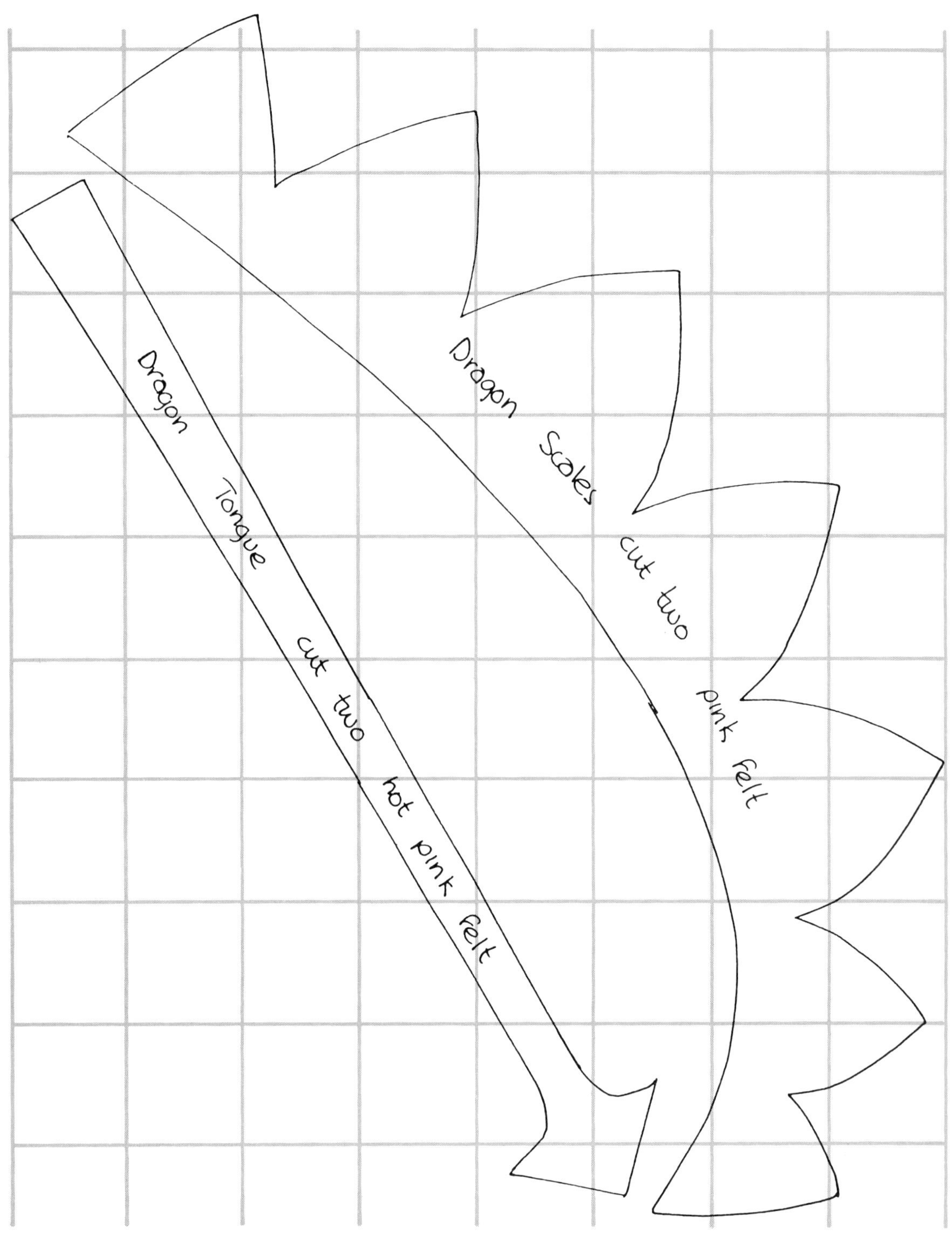

Illus. 98. Tongue and scales patterns for the Dragon (75 percent of original size)

Alvin the Alligator

Illus. 99

Materials: 15″ × 25″ green velour, felt, or velveteen
iron-on interfacing (optional)
13″ × 9″ dark-pink felt
2″ × 3″ light felt
2″ × 8″ white felt
1 pair of plastic lock-in frog eyes, 18mm
cardboard or plastic
tiny amount of polyester stuffing

Note: If you are using velour or another soft fabric for the alligator, you may wish to interface the body with iron-on interfacing before sewing.

BODY: Stitch the body pieces together, with the right sides facing, along front-seam A-B, and from the tip of the mouth around the top of the head along the back (C-D).

MOUTH: Baste the teeth into position along the edges of the mouth. Matching the notches on the mouth piece to points C-E-A-E on the mouth opening, stitch the mouth piece into the opening on the body, catching the teeth in your stitching.

TO FINISH: Glue the eyelids to the top of the eyes. Poke holes for the eye stems in the position indicated on the alligator body, and apply the eyes by pushing the stems through from the right side and securing them with lock washers. If you are unable to find plastic eyes, you can make eyes from felt by using the circle technique (page 8) and then attaching them after the alligator is completed. Now turn the puppet right side out, and apply the mouth lining according to the instructions on page 76.

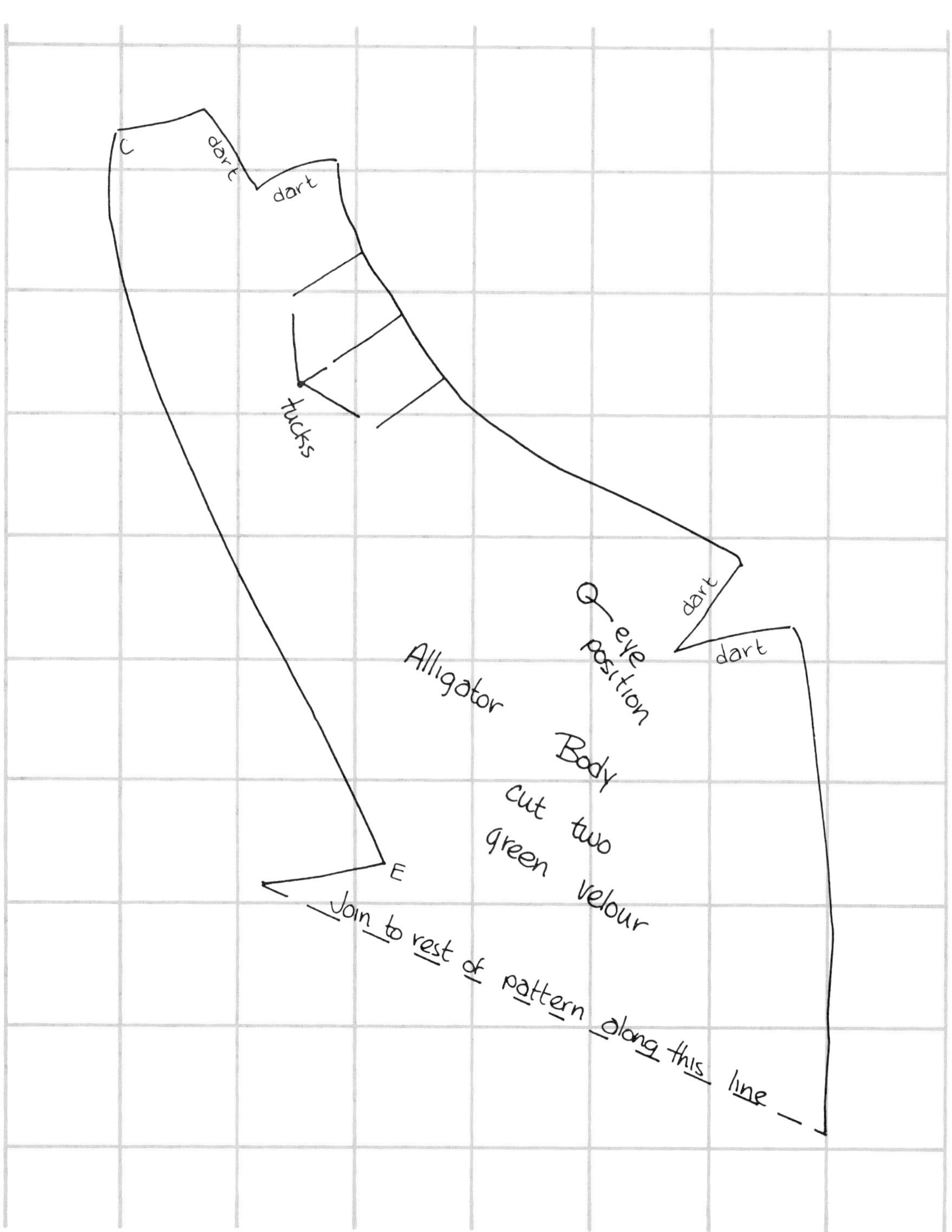

Illus. 100. Body pattern for Alvin the Alligator (75 percent of its original size)

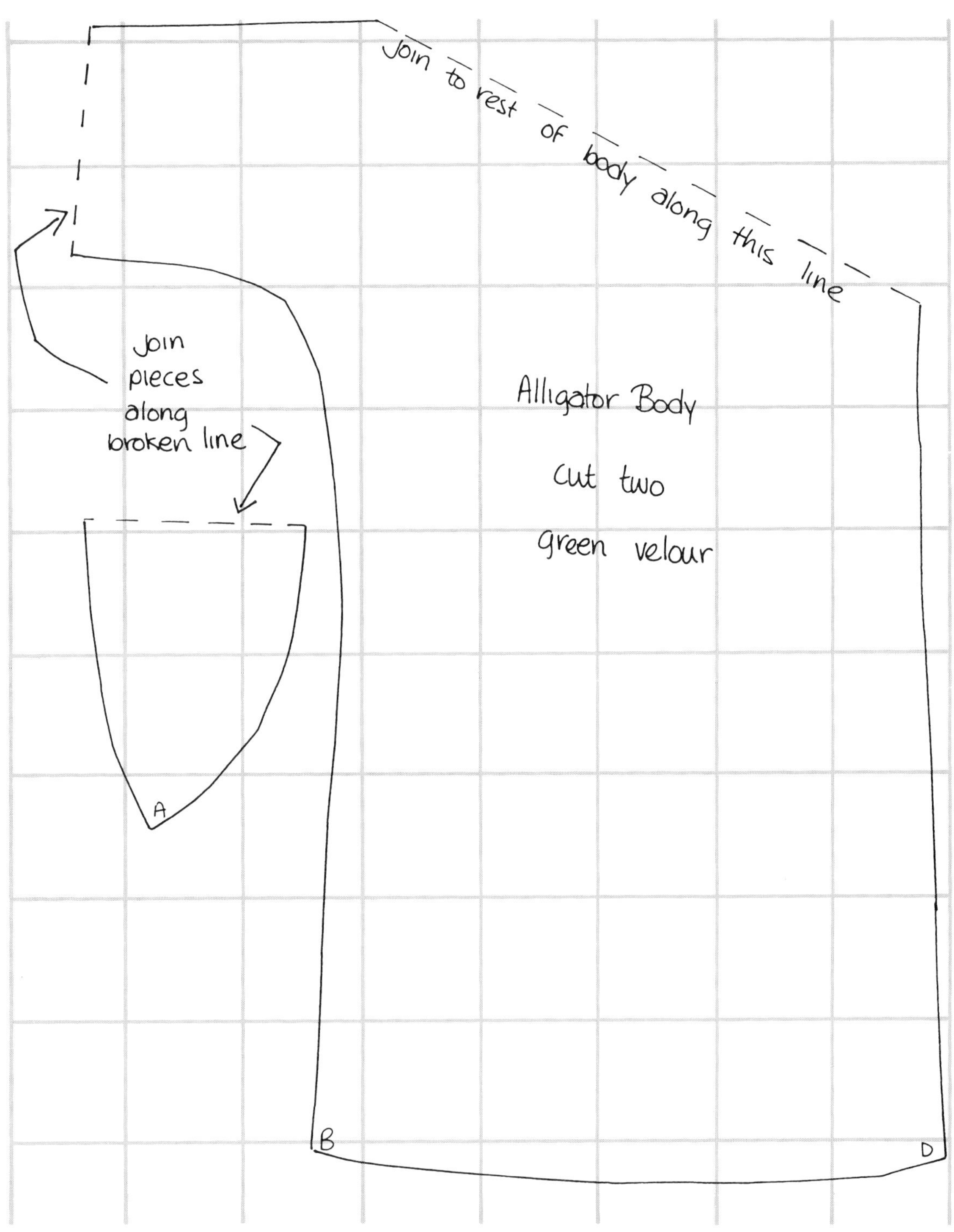

Illus. 101. Pattern for the rest of the Alligator's body (75 percent of its original size)

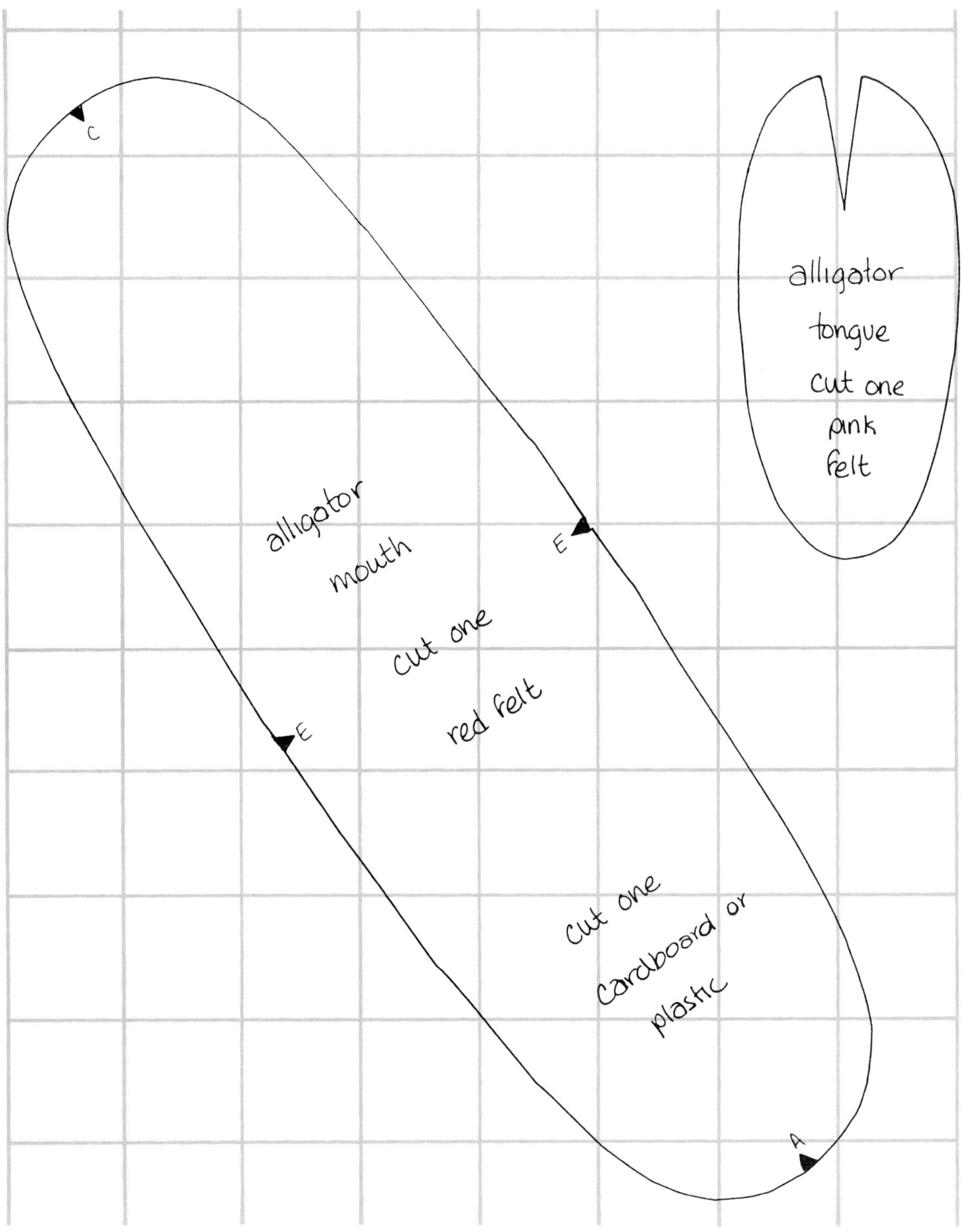

Illus. 102. Mouth and tongue patterns for the Alligator (75 percent of their original size)

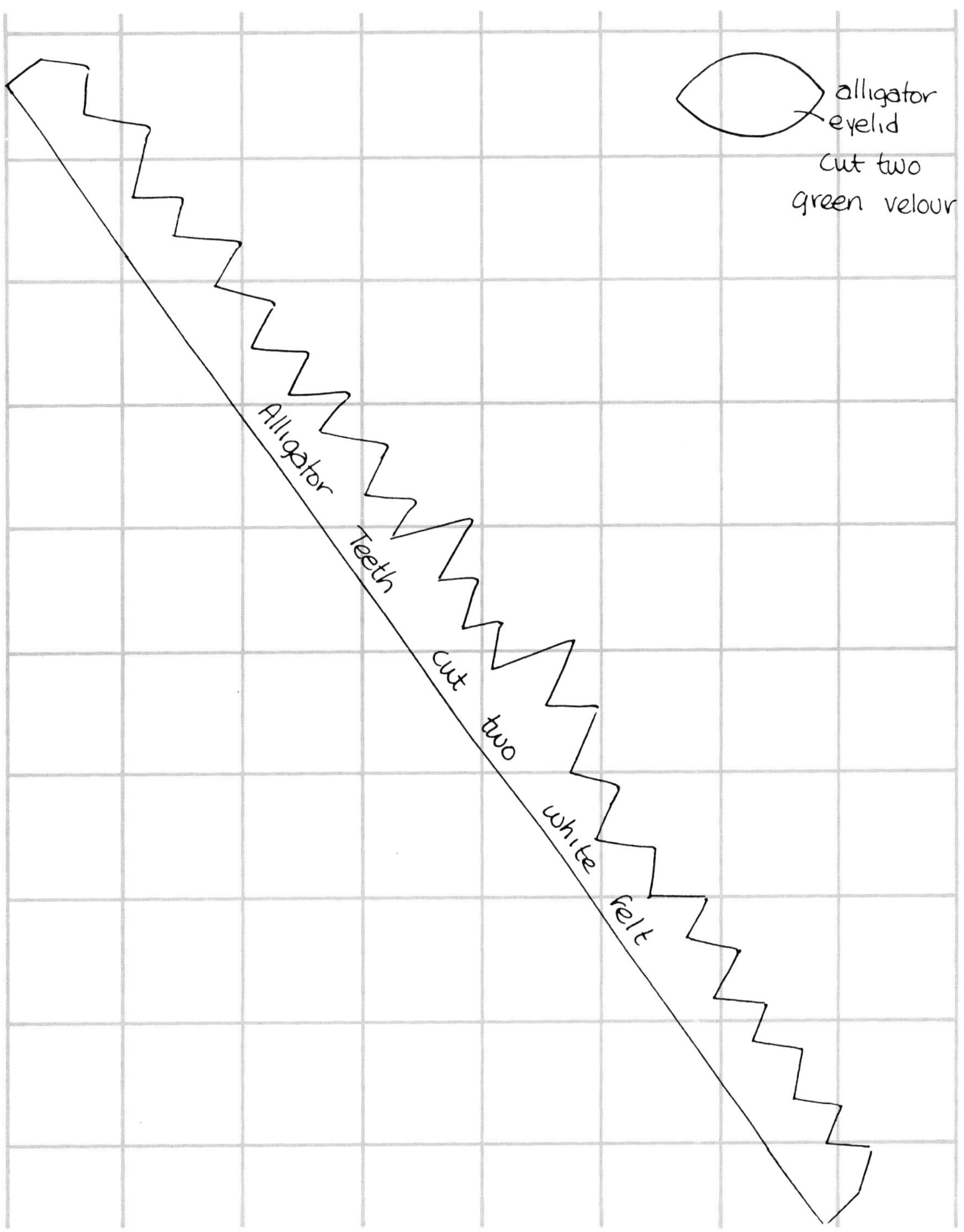

Illus. 103. Teeth and eyelid patterns for the Alligator (75 percent of their original size)

Dave and Donna, the Denim Twins

Illus. 104

Materials: 15″ × 45″ lightweight denim
6″ × 8″ long-pile red fur
6″ × 8″ short red fur
2 pairs of fancy plastic lock-in eyes, 18mm
5″ × 8″ red felt
two red sequins, 5mm
8″ × 36″ white T-shirt material
8″ × 8″ red-and-white bandana fabric
cardboard or plastic

Note: There are enough materials in this list to make both puppets.

ARMS: Stitch the arms together in pairs all around the edges, with the right sides facing, leaving the top straight edge open. Clip between the fingers and then turn the arms right side out. Stuff lightly to within 1 inch of the top, following the directions on page 7, and set aside.

EARS: Stitch the ears together in pairs all around the edges, with the right sides facing, leaving the top straight edge open. Turn the ears right side out and then slip them into the slits on the sides of the head so that they stick out. Stitch the slits closed so that the ears are caught in your stitching.

HAIR: With the wrong side of the hair piece facing the right side of the body, topstitch the hair to the body along the lower edge.

BODY: Insert the arms, facing forward, into slits A-B in the body, and stitch the slits closed, catching the tops of the arms in your stitching. Stitch darts in the top of the body pieces. With the right sides facing and matching all points, stitch the body sides together along all edges, leaving the body open along mouth-edges D-C-E and at the bottom. Matching points D-C-E-C on the body with the notches on the mouth piece, stitch the mouth into position. Poke holes where indicated on the body and then insert plastic eyes into position by pushing the stems through from the right side and fastening them with lock washers. Turn the body right side out and then turn up a narrow hem along the bottom of the puppet. Stitch.

MOUTH: Make the mouth lining from cardboard strengthened with interfacing or plastic, as described on page 76. Since the head is so large, you will need to attach pockets to the mouth lining so that the mouth can be manipulated effectively. Cut the pocket pieces from interfacing, and stitch them in position all around the mouth-lining piece, matching points J-K. Now insert the cardboard or plastic mouth into position, as described.

NOSE: Make the nose by using the circle technique (page 8) and then attach it to the front of the face with glue and stitching.

SHIRT: Stitch the sleeves to the shirt body all around the curved armhole, with the right sides facing and matching A-B-A. Refold the sleeves, with the right sides facing, so that the straight edges meet and then stitch along C-D. Stitch the middle-back seam along E-F. Hem the top and bottom of the T-shirt, and slip it on the puppet from the bottom. Make the kerchiefs by cutting the 8-inch bandana square in half diagonally; then fringe the edges. Tie the kerchief around the puppet's neck. Stitch sequins to the ears of the girl puppet to form earrings.

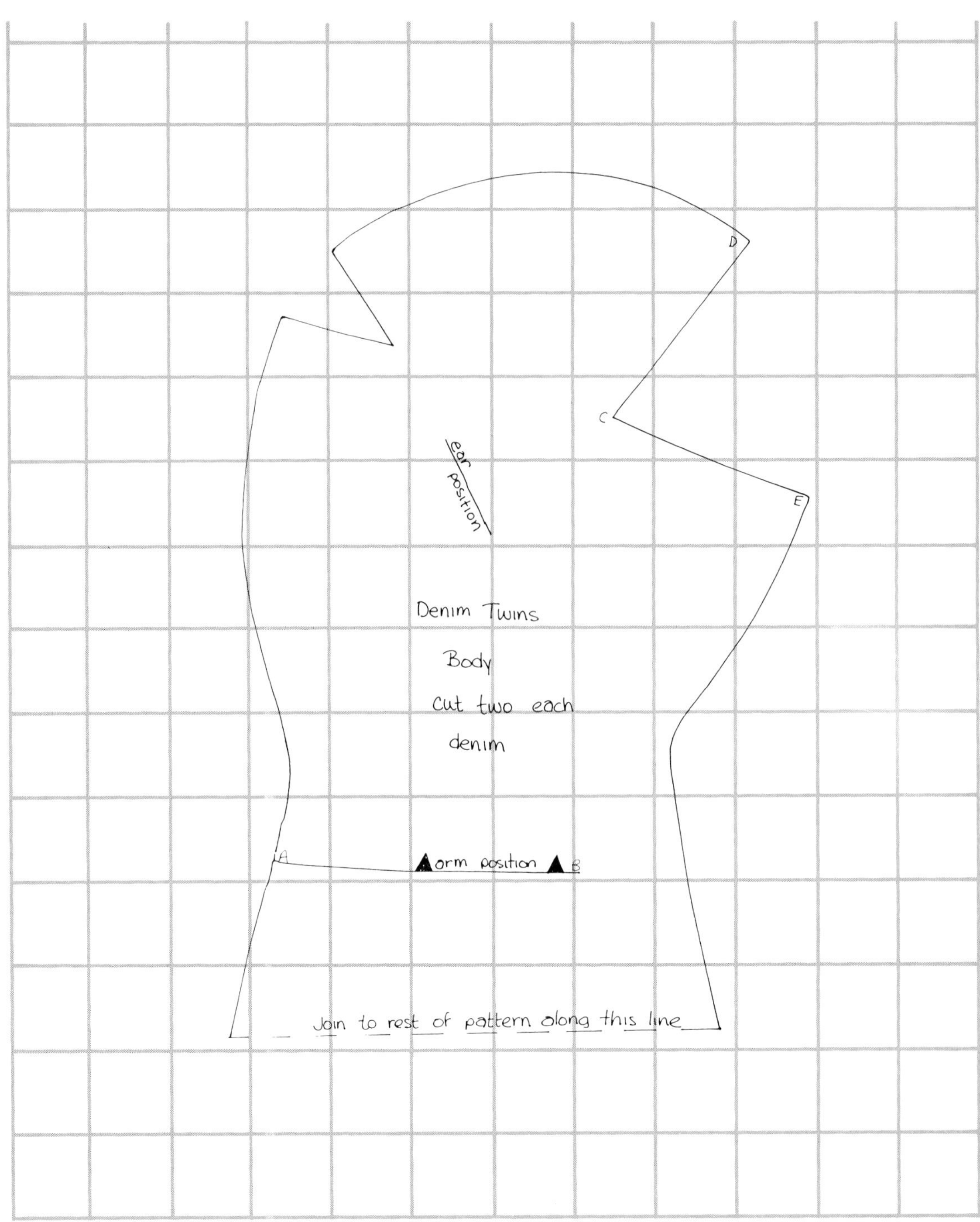

Illus. 105. Body pattern for the Denim Twins (50 percent of its original size)

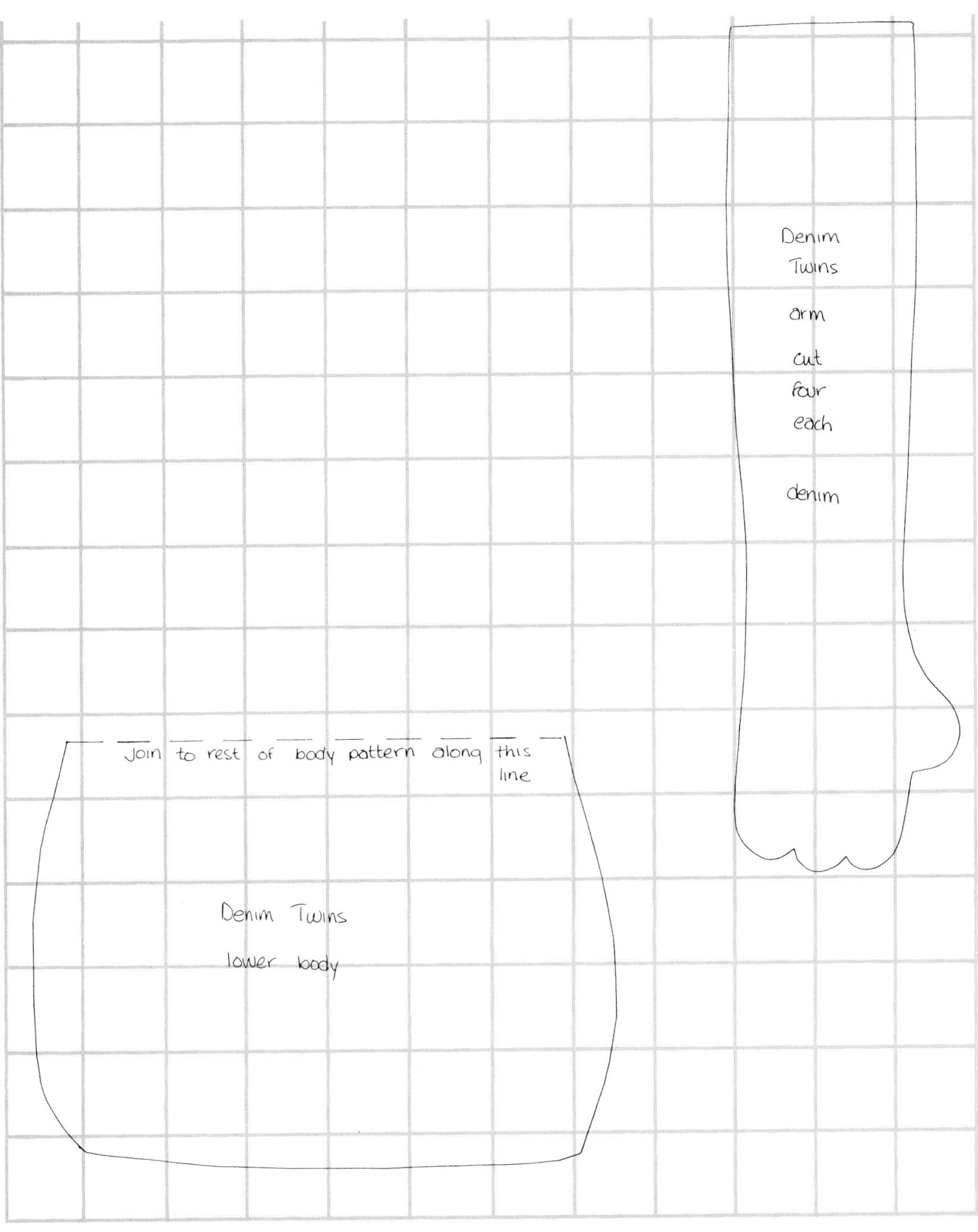

Illus. 106. Patterns for their lower body and arms (50 percent of their original size)

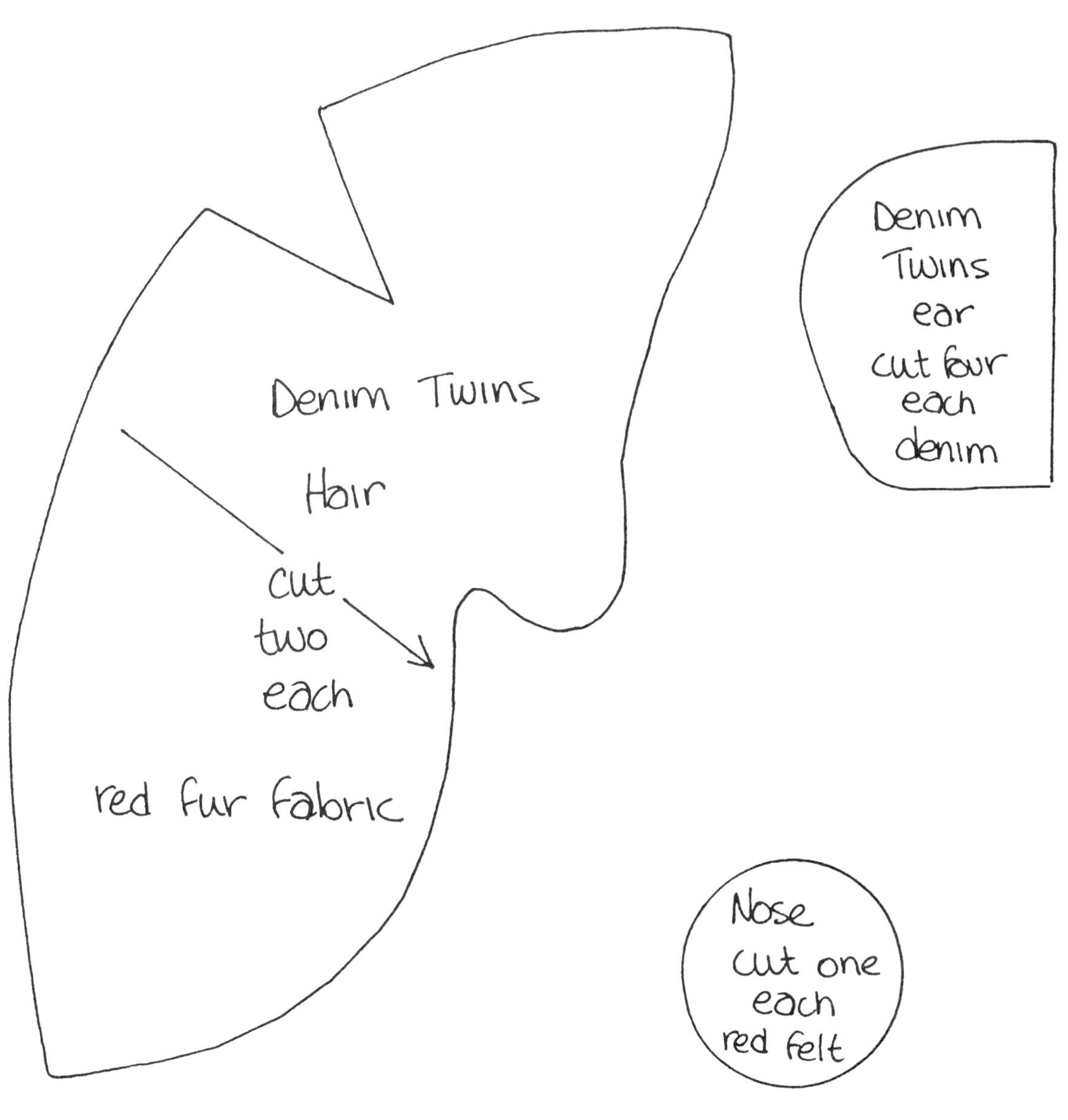

Illus. 107. Hair, ear, and nose patterns for the Denim Twins

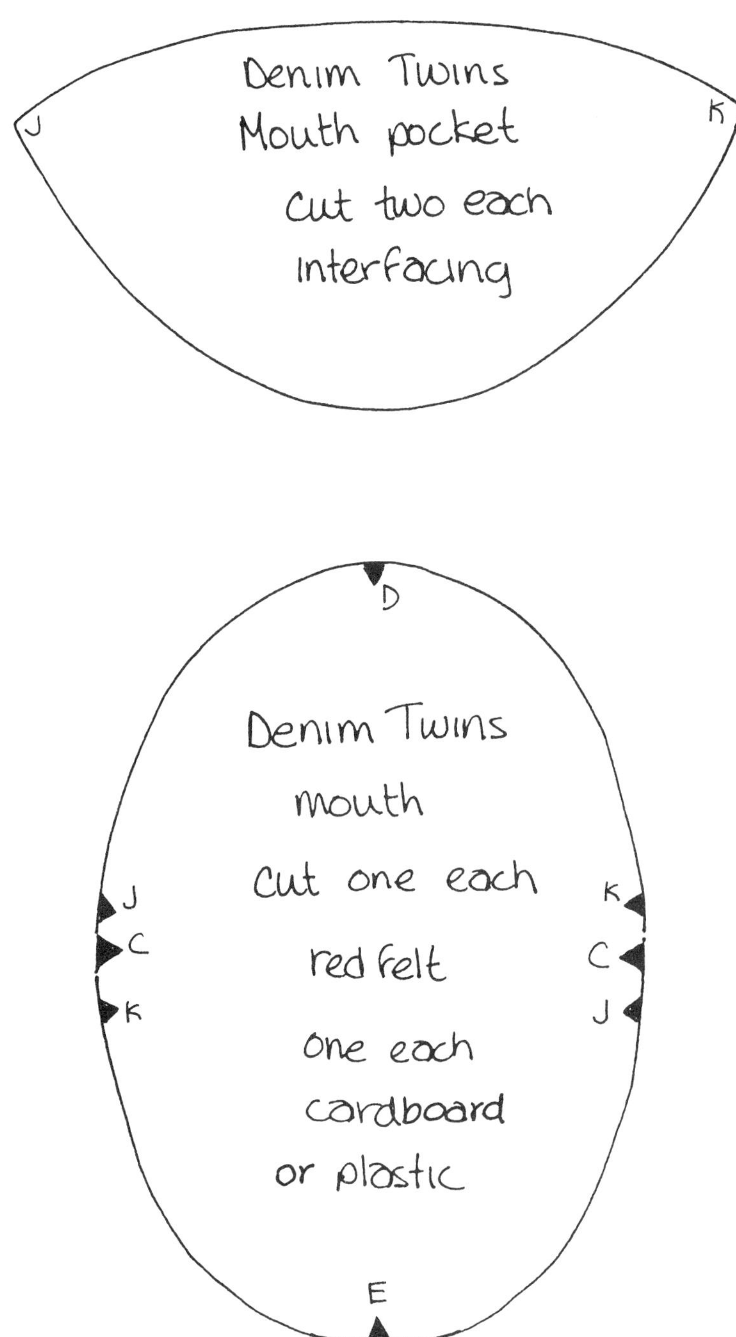

Illus. 108. Mouth and mouth pocket patterns for the Denim Twins

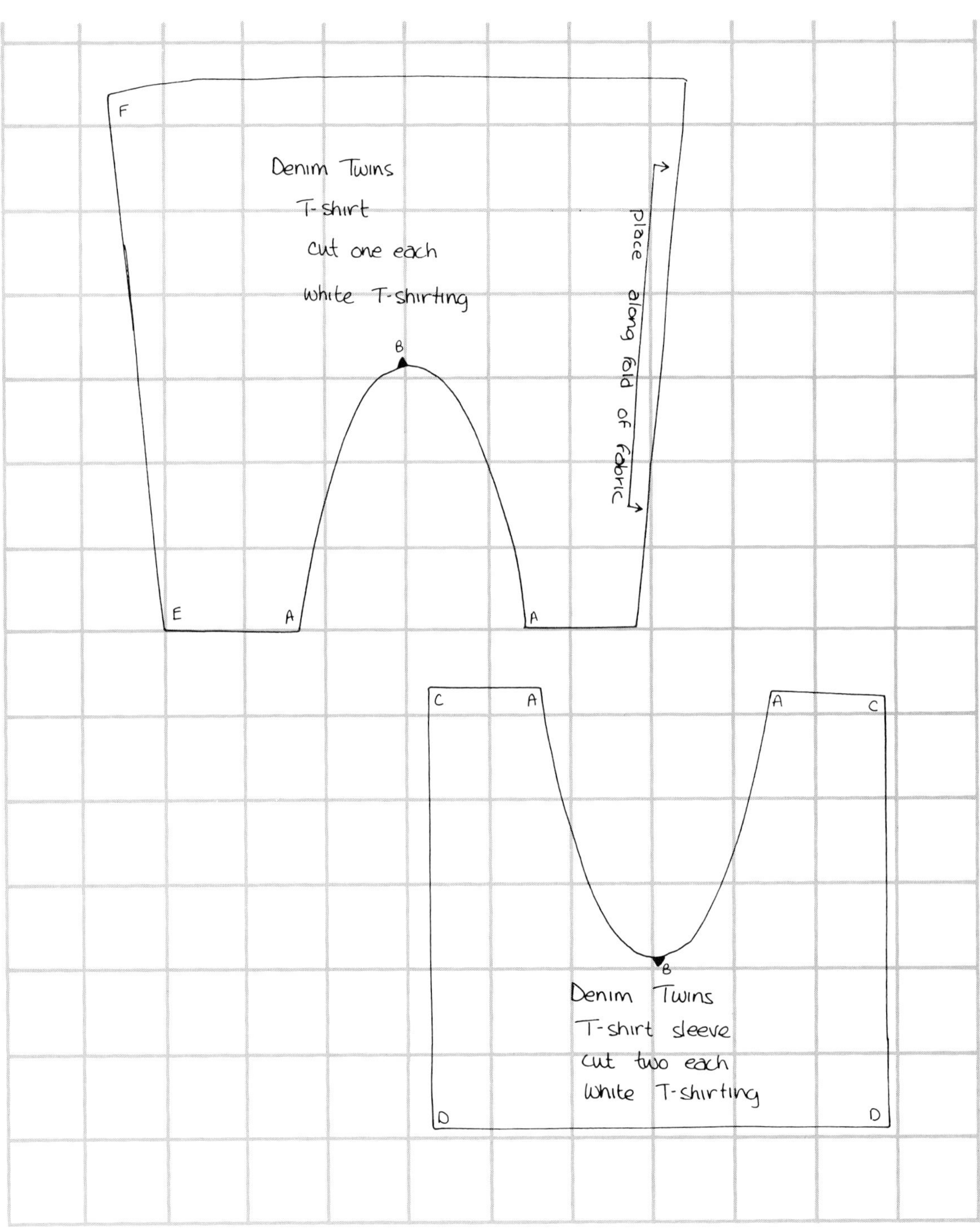

Illus. 109. T-shirt and T-shirt sleeve patterns for the Denim Twins (50 percent of their original size)

Magical Madame Sosostris, Gypsy

Illus. 110

Materials: 15″ × 20″ light-blue felt
6″ × 8″ long-pile blue fur
5″ × 8″ pink felt
small amounts of white and black felt
18″ × 36″ blue cotton print
13″ × 7″ blue cotton fabric
2 large flat gold sequins, 25mm
12″ × 36″ white cotton fabric
12″ × 12″ loosely woven blue fabric
small length of gold-colored chain
small amount of polyester stuffing
cardboard or plastic

ARMS: Stitch the hands together in pairs, with the right sides facing, between A and B. Open the hands out flat and stitch them to the bottom of the arms. Stitch all around the fingers and up the middle back of the arm, with the right sides facing, leaving the top straight edge open. Clip between the fingers and then turn the piece right side out. Stuff the hand lightly and then stitch across at the wrist to hold the stuffing in place. Set aside.

EARS: Stitch the ears together in pairs all around the edges, with the right sides facing, leaving the straight edge open. Turn the ears right side out and set them aside.

BUST: Make the breasts by stitching them in pairs, with the right sides facing, around the outer curved edge. With the right sides facing and matching points A-B, stitch the breasts into the opening on the body front.

BODY: Baste the arms and ears in the positions indicated on the body front. Matching all edges, stitch the body front to the body back along C-D, catching the ears and arms in your stitching.

HAIR: With the wrong side of the hair piece facing the right side of the body, topstitch the hair to the body along the lower edge of the hair piece.

LIPS: Stitch the two upper-lip pieces and the two lower-lip pieces together along the outer curved edges, with the right sides facing, leaving the inner curve open. Turn the lip piece right side out.

TO FINISH THE BODY: Stitch darts in the top of the body pieces. With the right sides facing and matching all points, stitch the body sides together along all edges, leaving the body open along mouth-edges E-F-G and at the bottom. Matching points E and G, stitch the lips into position along the edge of the mouth. Matching points E-F-G-F on the body with the notches on the mouth piece, stitch the mouth into position, catching the lips in your stitching. Turn the body right side out.

SHIRT: Stitch the sleeves to the shirt body all around the curved armhole, with the right sides facing and matching A-B-A. Refold the sleeves, with the right sides facing, so that the straight edges meet and then stitch along C-D. Stitch the middle-back seam along E-F. Fold $\frac{1}{4}$ inch along the top and sleeve edges towards the inside and then press. Run a gathering stitch around all three edges. Put the shirt onto the puppet, slipping it on from the bottom, but do not gather it to fit yet.

SKIRT: Fold the skirt in half, with the right sides facing, so that the short edges meet, and then stitch the back seam. Make a narrow hem around the bottom edge of the skirt. Run a gathering thread around the top edge of the skirt and pull it up to fit the bottom of the puppet body. Stitch the gathered skirt edge to the bottom of the body, with the right sides facing, catching the bottom of the shirt between. Prepare the body lining by folding it in half widthwise so that the shorter edges meet. Stitch this seam. Make a small rolled hem on one end of the lining tube. Insert the lining into the bottom of the puppet body, matching raw edges; then stitch the lining to the body along the previous line of stitching, catching the skirt and shirt in your stitching and leaving about 1 inch open. Turn the puppet right side out.

Tuck the lining to the inside of the puppet. Pull the gathered neck of the shirt to fit the neck of the puppet and then hand-stitch it in position along the gathered line, catching the lining to the inside of the puppet. Keep your hand inside the puppet during stitching to be sure that you don't stitch the neck closed. Lightly stuff the breasts and the lower body through the 1-inch opening, following the directions on page 7. Hand-stitch the opening closed. Gather the wrists of the shirt by pulling up on the gathering thread; then stitch them to the wrists of the puppet along the gathered line.

MOUTH: Make the mouth lining from cardboard strengthened with interfacing or plastic, as described on page 76. Since this puppet's head is so large, you will need to attach pockets to the mouth lining so that the mouth can be manipulated effectively. Cut pocket pieces from interfacing, and stitch them in position all around the mouth-lining piece, matching points J-K. Insert the cardboard or plastic mouth.

FACE: Make the nose by using the circle technique (page 8) and then attach it to the front of the face with glue and stitching. Glue the eyelids to the eye pieces and then make them with the circle technique. Glue the pupils to the eyes, and make "eyeliner" by outlining the edge of the eyelid with a black marker. Attach the eyes to the face with glue and stitching. Glue the lips to the front of the face and then color the cheeks lightly with pink or red crayon.

JEWELRY: Stitch spangles to the ears for earrings. Fasten the ends of the chain together and then slip it around the neck for a necklace. Catch the chain to the back of the neck with a couple of stitches.

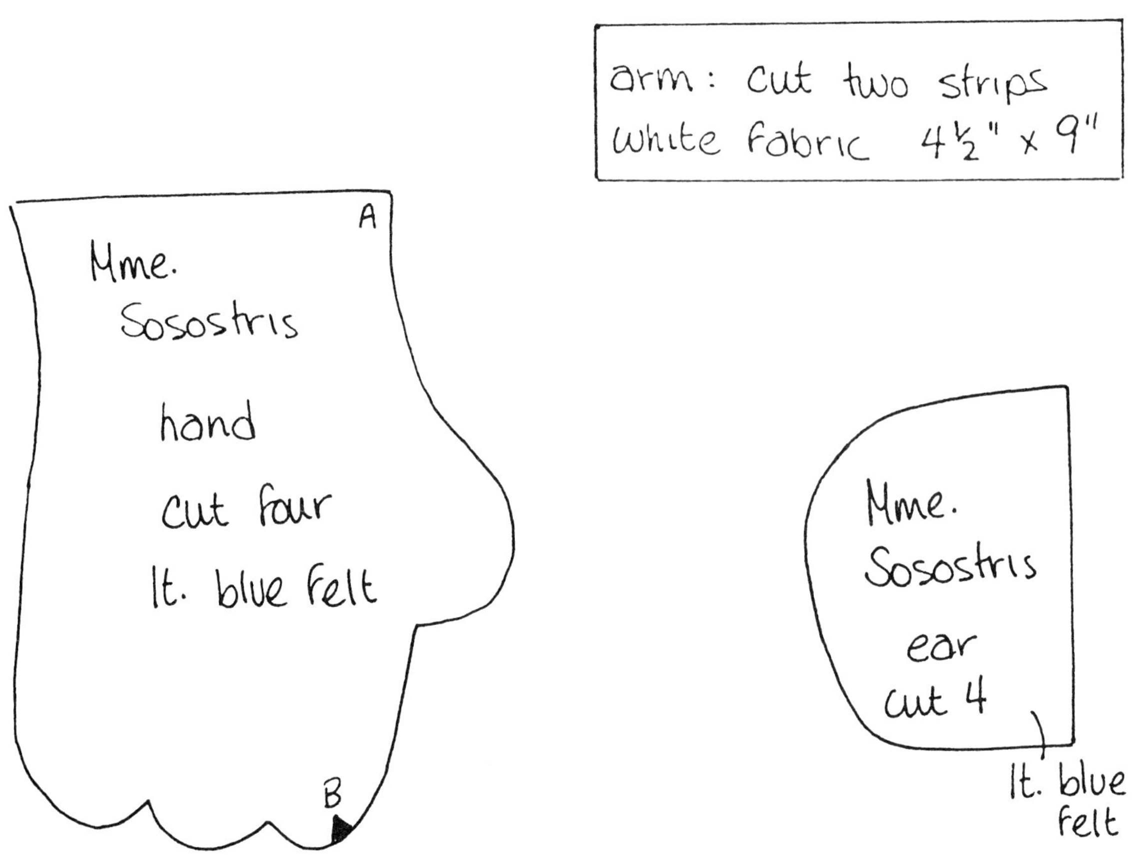

Illus. 111. Hand and ear patterns for Magical Madame Sosostris, and note regarding her arms

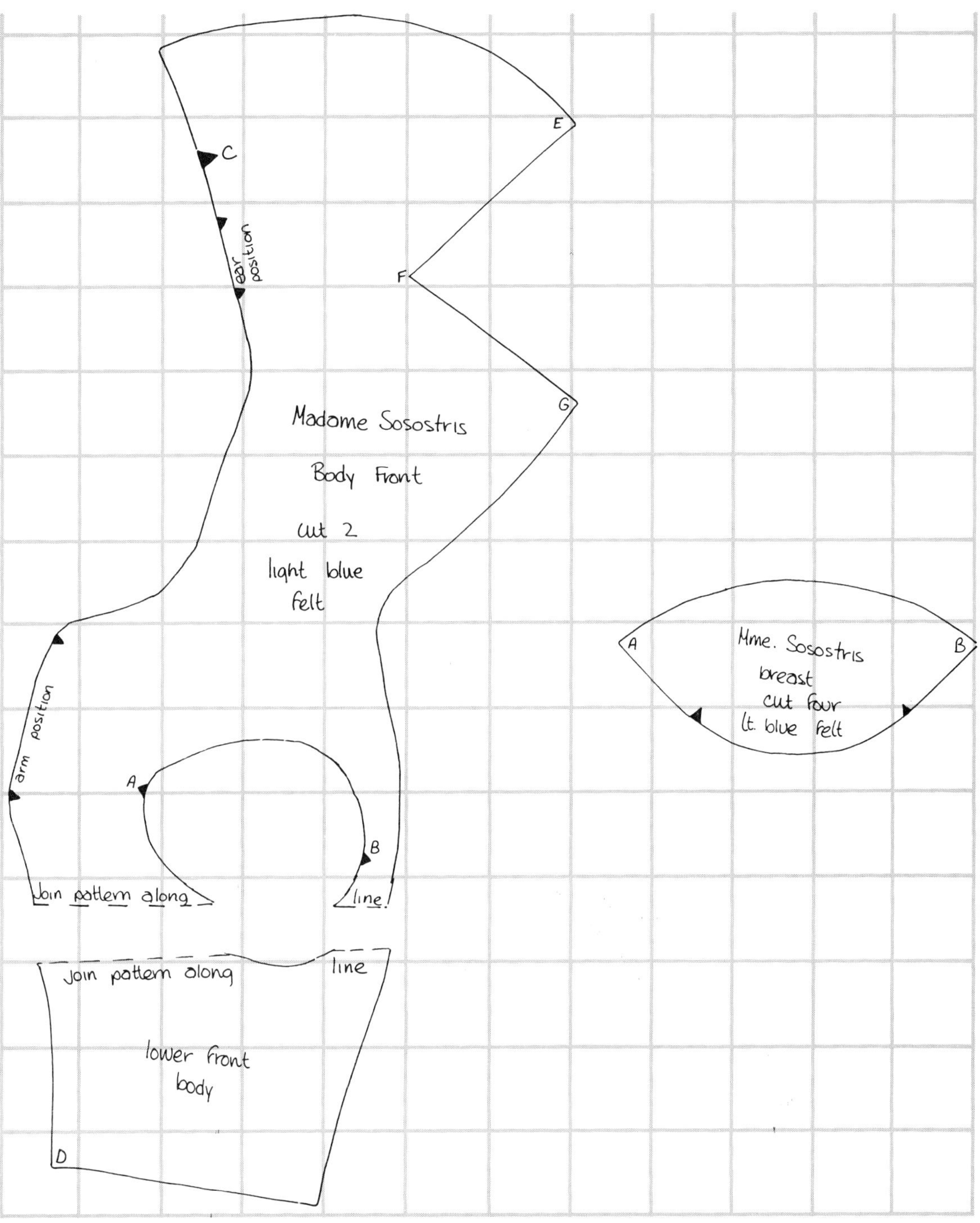

Illus. 112. Patterns for Madame Sosostris's body front, lower body front, and breast (50 percent of their original size)

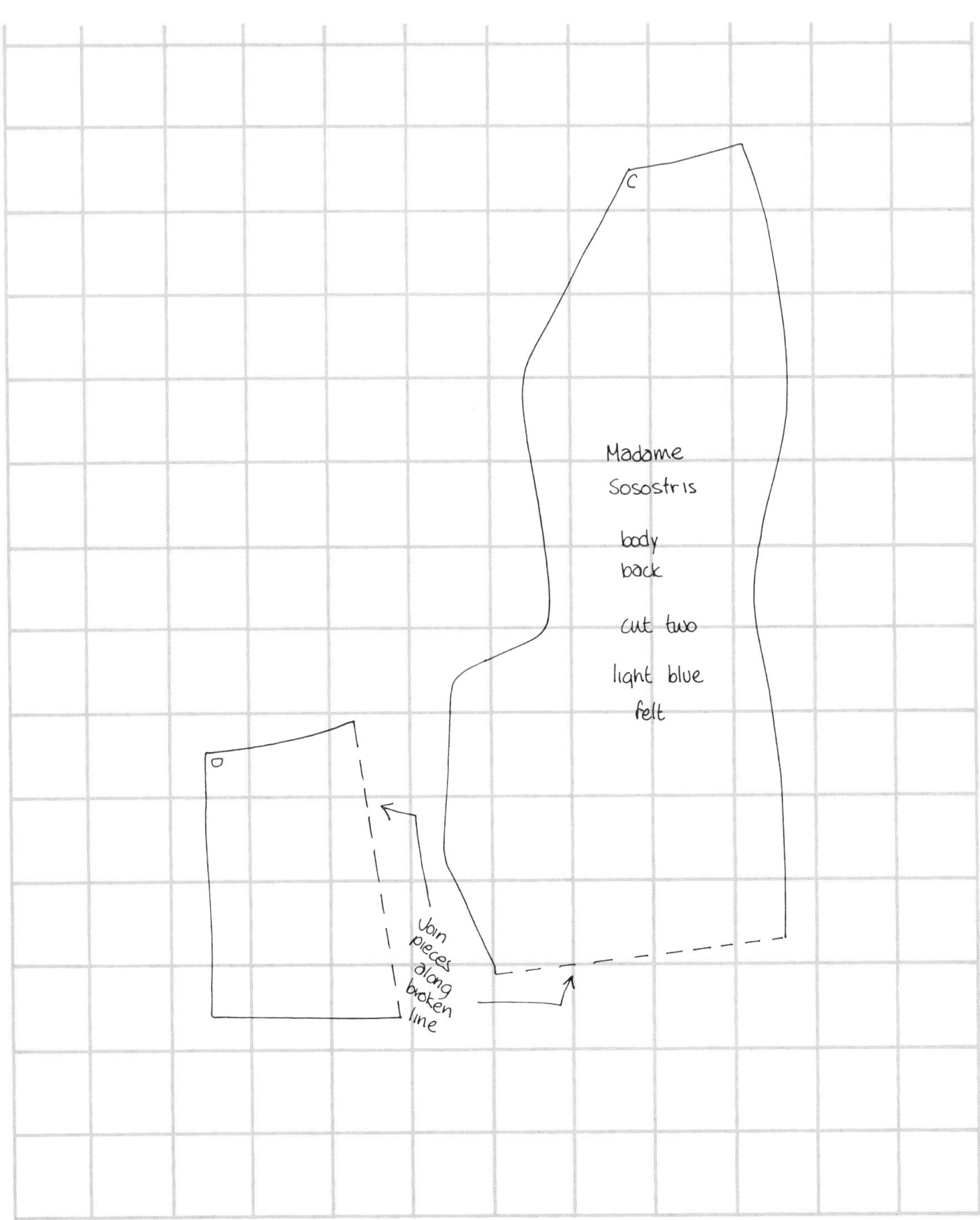

Illus. 113. Pattern for Madam Sosostris's body back (50 percent of its original size)

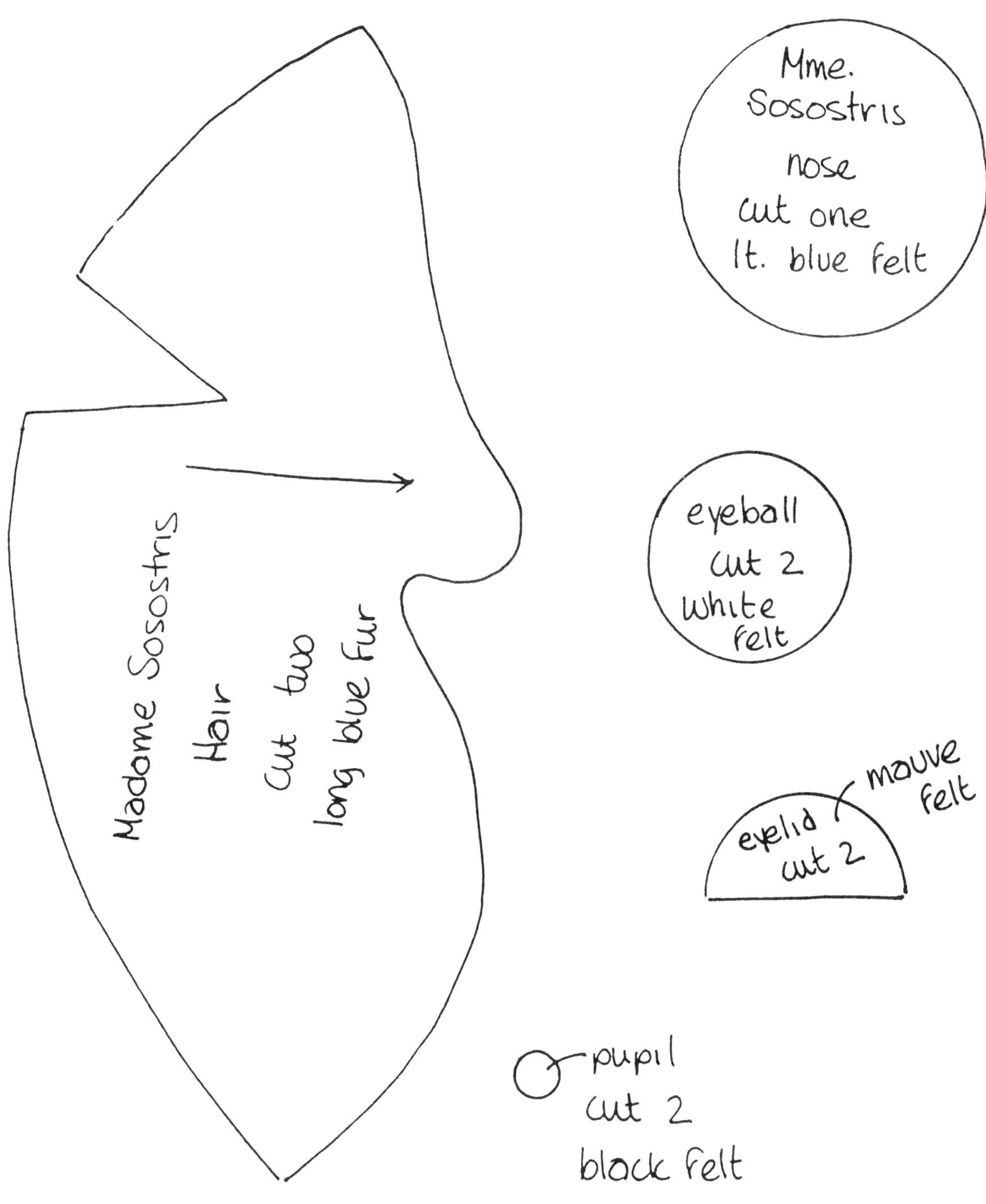

Illus. 114. Hair, nose, and eye patterns for Madame Sosostris

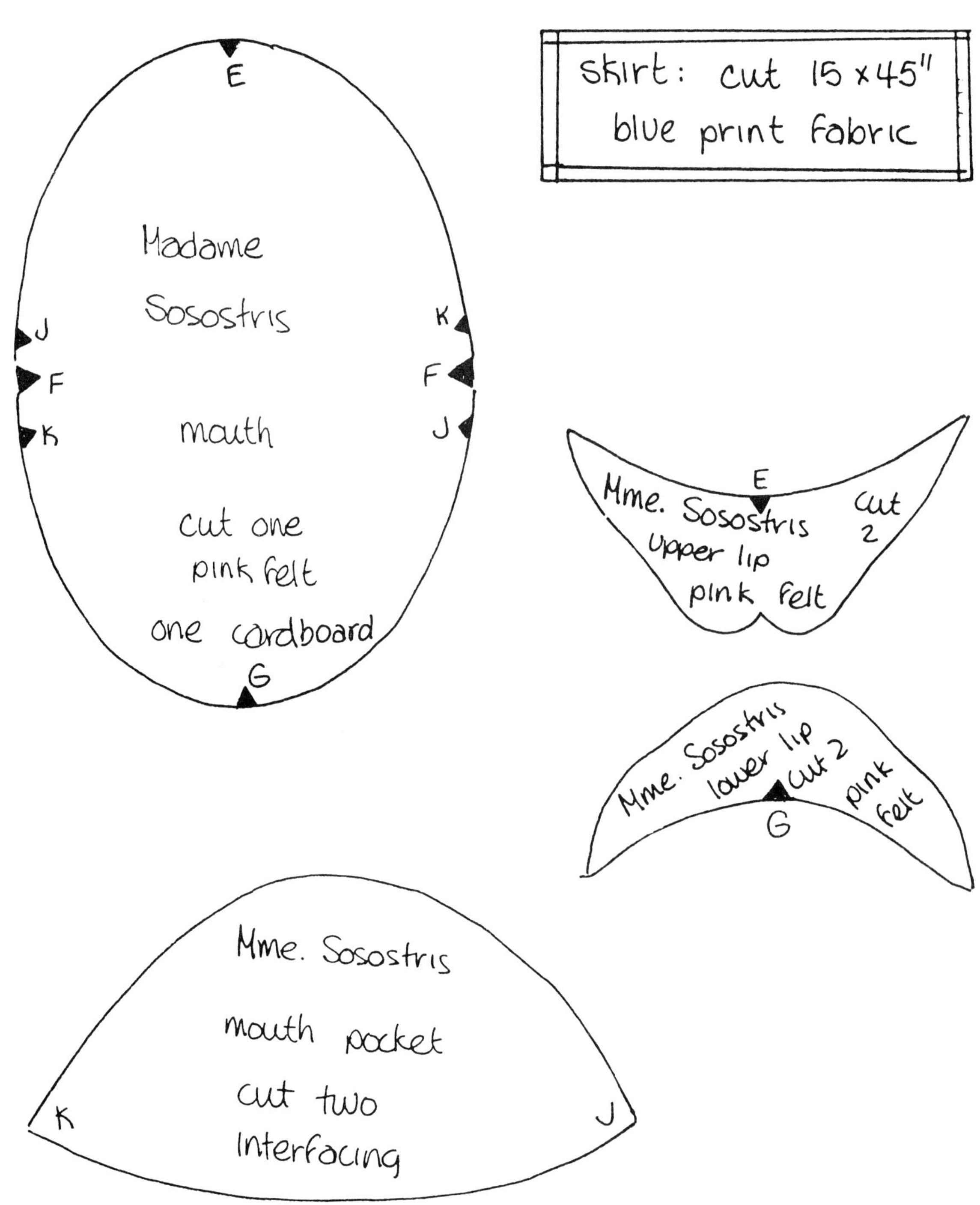

Illus. 115. Mouth, mouth pocket, and lips patterns for Madame Sosostris, and note about her skirt

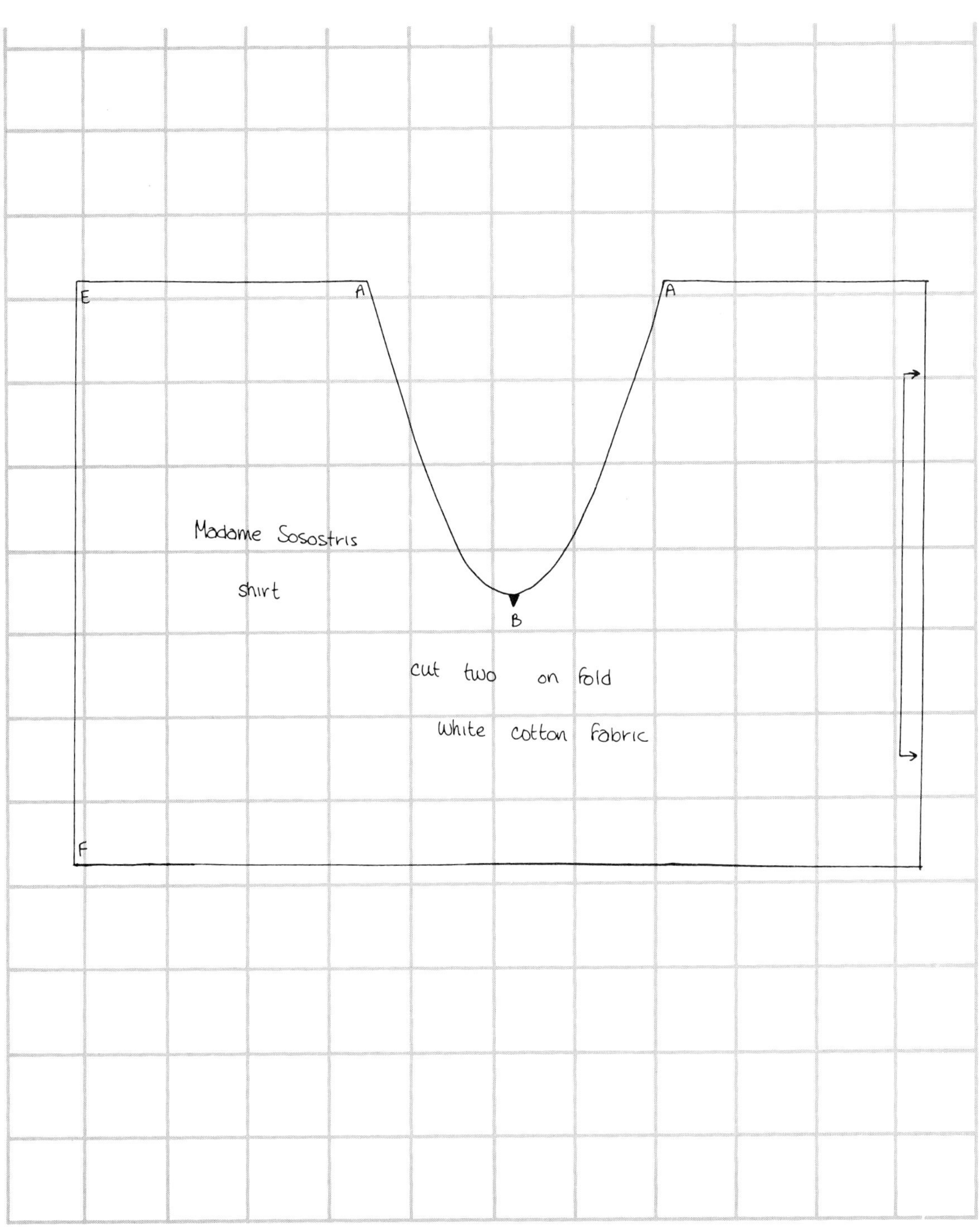

Illus. 116. Shirt pattern for Madame Sosostris (50 percent of its original size)

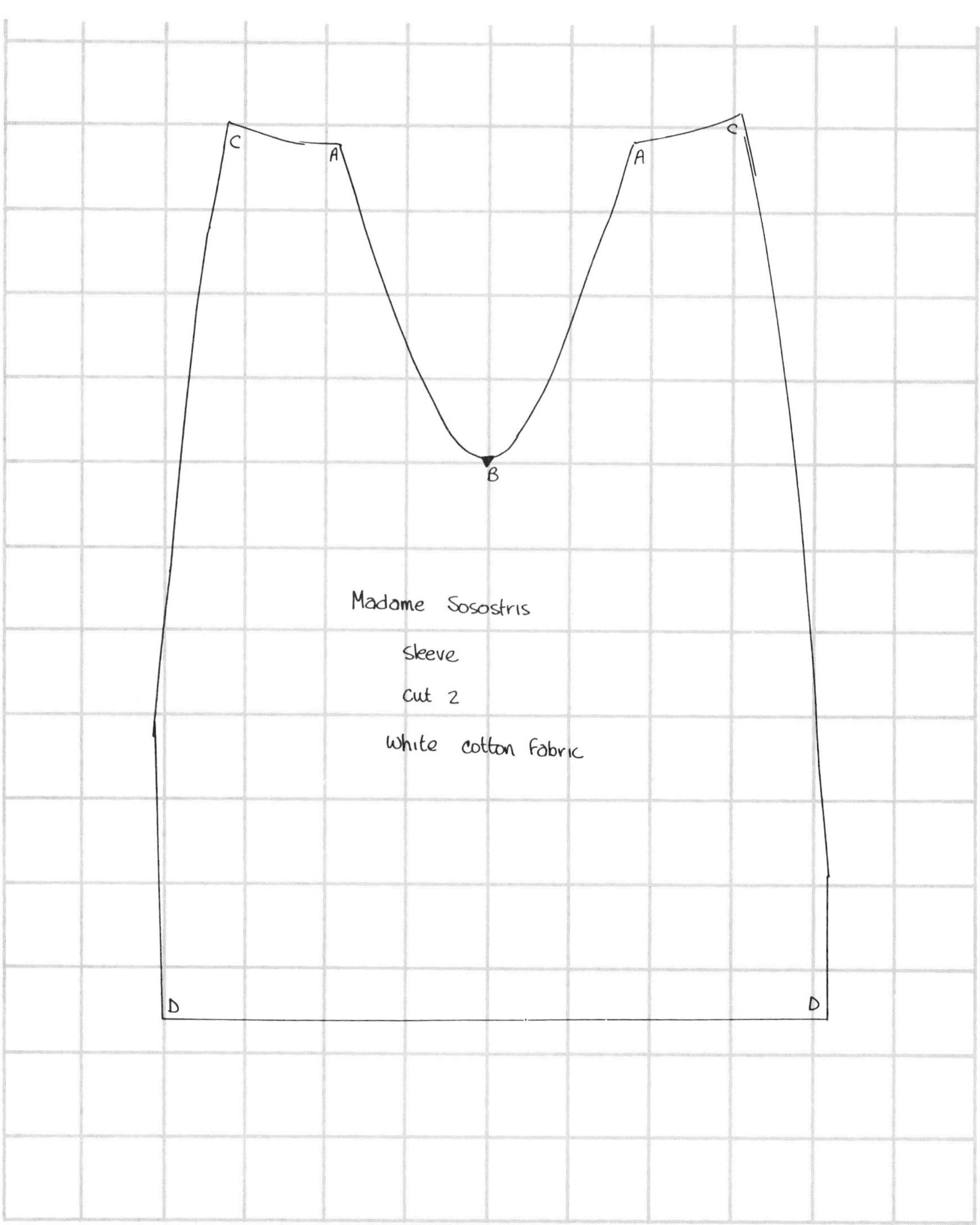

Illus. 117. Sleeve pattern for Madame Sosostris (50 percent of its original size)

METRIC EQUIVALENCY CHART

MM—MILLIMETRES   CM—CENTIMETRES

INCHES TO MILLIMETRES AND CENTIMETRES

INCHES	MM	CM	INCHES	CM	INCHES	CM
⅛	3	0.3	9	22.9	30	76.2
¼	6	0.6	10	25.4	31	78.7
⅜	10	1.0	11	27.9	32	81.3
½	13	1.3	12	30.5	33	83.8
⅝	16	1.6	13	33.0	34	86.4
¾	19	1.9	14	35.6	35	88.9
⅞	22	2.2	15	38.1	36	91.4
1	25	2.5	16	40.6	37	94.0
1¼	32	3.2	17	43.2	38	96.5
1½	38	3.8	18	45.7	39	99.1
1¾	44	4.4	19	48.3	40	101.6
2	51	5.1	20	50.8	41	104.1
2½	64	6.4	21	53.3	42	106.7
3	76	7.6	22	55.9	43	109.2
3½	89	8.9	23	58.4	44	111.8
4	102	10.2	24	61.0	45	114.3
4½	114	11.4	25	63.5	46	116.8
5	127	12.7	26	66.0	47	119.4
6	152	15.2	27	68.6	48	121.9
7	178	17.8	28	71.1	49	124.5
8	203	20.3	29	73.7	50	127.0

YARDS TO METRES

YARDS	METRES	YARDS	METRES	YARDS	METRES	YARDS	METRES	YARDS	METRES
⅛	0.11	2⅛	1.94	4⅛	3.77	6⅛	5.60	8⅛	7.43
¼	0.23	2¼	2.06	4¼	3.89	6¼	5.72	8¼	7.54
⅜	0.34	2⅜	2.17	4⅜	4.00	6⅜	5.83	8⅜	7.66
½	0.46	2½	2.29	4½	4.11	6½	5.94	8½	7.77
⅝	0.57	2⅝	2.40	4⅝	4.23	6⅝	6.06	8⅝	7.89
¾	0.69	2¾	2.51	4¾	4.34	6¾	6.17	8¾	8.00
⅞	0.80	2⅞	2.63	4⅞	4.46	6⅞	6.29	8⅞	8.12
1	0.91	3	2.74	5	4.57	7	6.40	9	8.23
1⅛	1.03	3⅛	2.86	5⅛	4.69	7⅛	6.52	9⅛	8.34
1¼	1.14	3¼	2.97	5¼	4.80	7¼	6.63	9¼	8.46
1⅜	1.26	3⅜	3.09	5⅜	4.91	7⅜	6.74	9⅜	8.57
1½	1.37	3½	3.20	5½	5.03	7½	6.86	9½	8.69
1⅝	1.49	3⅝	3.31	5⅝	5.14	7⅝	6.97	9⅝	8.80
1¾	1.60	3¾	3.43	5¾	5.26	7¾	7.09	9¾	8.92
1⅞	1.71	3⅞	3.54	5⅞	5.37	7⅞	7.20	9⅞	9.03
2	1.83	4	3.66	6	5.49	8	7.32	10	9.14

Index